W9-DAJ-895

Contents

Acknowledgments

We would like to express our gratitude to President Dr. Jerry Gallentine and to the community of National American University for their commitment to the curriculum of The Pacific Institute and for their support of our careers and ideas.

We also thank Lou and Diane Tice, founders of The Pacific Institute, for their outstanding curriculum, a commitment to helping change lives and social systems for the betterment of all. Thanks to Dr. Joe Pace, who was the change agent for many.

We also want to thank Randy Haubner, our Acquisitions Editor at JIST Publishing, who saw the value in this work and created the team to make it happen. We share our success with this team of professionals, including Robin Drake, Barb Terry, Linda Seifert, Aleata Howard, and Jeanne Clark. They reconfirmed for us the power of synergy in action. Finally, we thank Michael Farr, owner of JIST Publishing, who allowed this project to become a reality.

~The Authors

Karine Blackett and Patricia Weiss

College Success Guide

Top 12 Secrets for Student Success

Karine Blackett and Patricia Weiss

jist Works

America's Career Publisher®

College Success Guide
© 2005 by Karine Blackett and Patricia Weiss

Published by JIST Works, an imprint of JIST Publishing
7321 Shadeland Station, Suite 200
Indianapolis, IN 46256-3923
Phone: 800-648-JIST   Fax: 877-454-7839   E-mail: info@jist.com

Visit our Web site at www.jist.com for more information on JIST, free job search information, tables of contents, sample pages, and ordering information on our many products! Please call our Sales Department at 800-648-5478 for a free catalog and more information.

Acquisitions Editor: Randy Haubner
Development Editors: Robin Drake, Barb Terry Howe
Proofreader: Linda Seifert
Cover Designer: Trudy Coler
Interior Designer: Aleata Halbig
Indexer: Kelly D. Henthorne

Printed in the United States of America.
12 11 10 09   9 8 7 6 5 4

Library of Congress Cataloging-in-Publication Data

Blackett, Karine.
  College success guide : top 12 secrets for student success / Karine Blackett and Patricia Weiss.
     p. cm.
  Includes bibliographical references and index.
  ISBN 1-59357-130-5
  1. Study skills--Handbooks, manuals, etc. 2. College student orientation--Handbooks, manuals,
etc. 3. Success--Handbooks, manuals, etc. I. Weiss, Patricia, 1951- II. Title.
  LB2395.B317 2005
  378.1'70281--dc22
                                        2004016956

We have been careful to provide accurate information in this book, but it is possible that errors and omissions have been introduced. Please consider this in making any career plans or other important decisions. Trust your own judgment above all else and in all things.

Trademarks: All brand names and product names used in this book are trade names, service marks, trademarks, or registered trademarks of their respective owners.

ISBN 978-1-59357-130-6

Preface

Welcome! We are pleased to have you pick up this book. You are holding the first edition of the *College Success Guide: Top 12 Secrets for Student Success*. We have taken the best practices of college students from around the country and world and compiled them for you along with useful tips, tools, and suggestions to make your college experience meet and exceed your wildest expectations. We are in the success business and want you to save time, money, and heartache by having these best practices at your fingertips.

Our book covers the experts' advice found to be truly helpful by students—from the nontraditional students to those entering college from high school. Many of these students have families and full-time jobs, and yet they found ways to have dynamic college experiences and succeed. That is our hope for you as well. Use these tools, not because the experts say they work, but because other learners found they work!

One outstanding feature of this book is that it offers more than one way to win. Take Chapter 11, "Success Secret 11: Time Management," for example. The chapter presents many excellent tools to improve planning one's time. By providing different strategies, we have made it possible for you to tailor a time-management system that actually works for you. If you are a procrastinator, you can use tools designed to motivate you; if you are a chronic planner, you can learn to bring more flexibility and synergy into your life so that you get more accomplished with ease. In any case, you can pull from many secrets of student success to get the most out of your education.

We have heard students say, "I have been trying so hard!" and what we say to you is, "Stop trying so hard." That is like rock climbing without using any of the tools already invented to help you make it to the top of the mountain relatively painlessly and actually have fun in the process. Tools also exist for you to get your diploma without spending your energy on "not knowing how to do it more easily." This book will help you succeed in college more easily and with better results.

We have incorporated digital media into this text, as well as interactive guided exercises, for you to find more success tools that are unique to you and your needs.

A first edition will always have room for new suggestions, and we hope that you take the time to write to us and give us your feedback on how we can make the best practices even better the next time around.

Introduction

College Success Guide: Top 12 Secrets for Student Success can help you become more efficient and effective in studying. The 12 secrets it offers have enabled thousands of students to achieve far more than they originally believed possible. The two educators who serve as your guide to grasping those secrets are Karine Blackett and Patricia Weiss.

Karine Beth Blackett's interest in higher education has taken her around the world: She studied at the University of Malta and worked in Kenya, Africa, through her undergraduate degree with The University of Minnesota. She holds an English Language Teaching Certificate from New School University in New York, and she taught English as a second language in Japan. Karine earned an M.S. from Colorado State University in Student Affairs in Higher Education.

Karine is Career Services Manager for the Distance Learning Campus of National American University, based in South Dakota, where she teaches the skills she covers in detail in this book. Karine also contributed to the third edition of *The Very Quick Job Search,* also by JIST Publishing. As an educator, Karine teaches career development courses online, as well as Strategies for Success, which covers the principles and universal laws used by high-performance people and those designing their lives by intent and not by default. Karine is a certified Success Coach and is currently working on her own Ph.D. through Capella University Online.

Patricia Weiss earned a B.S. in business administration in 1990 and a B.S. in accounting in 1992. She has been a paraprofessional in library services for 12 years, an experience she has found very rewarding. She also has been an adjunct faculty member at National American University for 12 years. Patricia is a member of the American Library Association and the Mountain Plains Library Association, and is a facilitator for The Pacific Institute.

Patricia was an academic coach for four years, has given instruction to hundreds of students in library research, and has facilitated the Strategies for Success class at National American University for the past 12 years.

How to Read This Guide

You do not need to read the chapters in this book in any order unless you are using it for a classroom text and your instructor has given you assignments. Otherwise, we suggest that you look over the Table of Contents to see which chapters you are most drawn to as well as which chapters you have the most resistance to reading. It may very well be that the ones that you would like to dismiss or skip are precisely the ones that you need the most at this point in your life. With this principle in mind, you may want to go to those chapters first to see what you are avoiding and what they can bring into your life in a more positive way.

What Tools to Use

First, we suggest that you get a highlighter and mark the tips or best practices that you feel you can benefit the most from and do not want to forget. You may also want to highlight the Web site addresses that you want to visit, so they are easy to find. (You may want to use a second color for highlighting these items.)

Another tool is to complete the assignments in the chapters so you can actually see some benefits of the suggestions. There is a success principle behind this thinking. If you continue to plot out your life as you have been doing, you will continue to get the same results. Now, many of you may be thinking that your way has served you just fine, and you do not want to rock the boat or get out of your comfort zone, so to speak. Well, we want you to know that if you are willing to take a new approach, two wonderful things will happen, even if you later decide to go back to your old ways of managing your college experience. First, you will shake up things in your subconscious enough that new ideas and creative energy will start to flow in other areas of your life. (This is also a reason you might want to drive a new way home now and then, or do something you usually don't do, like attending some social function.) The second reason for trying a new tool or approach is that you may find that you had a blind spot in your old way, and can now save more time or get more accomplished in less time. For these reasons we suggest that you try a new approach or success tool for three weeks before you make a decision.

What the 12 Secrets Offer

The *College Success Guide* was designed to give college and university students like you tried-and-true tools that you can implement on your own and get actual results in a short amount of time. It is like having your own personal success coach guide you through the things highly successful students do. Following are some of the success secrets you will find in the chapters.

Chapter 1 Success Secret #1: Study Skills

This chapter teaches you what high-performance learners do to study effectively for results. For example, you will learn how to increase your reading retention so you can spend less time reading and rereading the material. Other tools include learning how use chunking, symbols, and lists, as well as other study skills best practices.

Chapter 2 Success Secret #2: Test-Taking Skills

Learn how to manage test anxiety—intelligence is largely what you can do effectively when you are under stress. Even if you have the knowledge, if you suffer from anxiety, your results can still be poor. You will also learn the test-taking secrets that student use to improve their performance on examinations.

Chapter 3 Success Secret #3: Perception, Learning Styles, and Personality

Discover an important, but often-overlooked truth: Not everyone learns the same way. Sometimes a teacher teaches using a method that is not conducive to the way you learn. If you struggle to understand the materials, the problem may not be that you are not smart enough to master the topic. It may be that you learn better when you approach the material from a different angle. So are you doomed? Not at all. This chapter will help you identify how you learn best, so you can get the most out of your classes regardless of how the material is presented.

Chapter 4 Success Secret #4: Organization

Is there a way to become organized so you get better results in college? You bet there is. Chapter 4 gives you the secrets and best practices of students that use certain organization techniques for better performance.

Chapter 5 Success Secret #5: Attitude

Attitude, it has been said, is the single most important key to your success in any area of your life. Like William James said, "A human being can alter his life by altering his attitude." And we are not talking about becoming a syrupy happy Pollyanna. This chapter teaches you how to use the power of your thoughts and attitude to get the results you seek in your college experience. You can use these simple tools and get better results immediately.

Chapter 6 Success Secret #6: Goal Setting

Unique to humans is the fact that without goals there is, in essence, no life. In effect, you have been using goal setting either by purposeful design or by default. You will know if you have been setting goals by default because you do not have the things that you hoped for, wanted, and desperately desired. Rather, you find yourself wondering why others seem to have more or do more than you have or do. You also may feel that you try hard, often really hard, with little result or with challenges. If these statements sound familiar, then this chapter is for you.

Chapter 7 Success Secret #7: Basic Research Skills

Just as most of us need a recipe to make a terrific gourmet dish, most students need a recipe to do excellent research. Without such a recipe, students may be tempted to spend a great deal of time and energy gathering data and end up with very little material, or a great deal of poor-quality material. This chapter takes you beyond an Internet search and gives you simple ways to do awesome research. This chapter is your personal recipe to doing great research.

Chapter 8 Success Secret #8: Research Papers

Much like the recipe for successful research, there are best practices for outstanding research papers. This chapter gives you the best tips and tools for writing excellent research papers. It also shares the URLs of Web sites that walk you through the process. In essence, you will have a coach by your side to help you make the process of writing a research paper less like a chore, and more like baking a cake (and a boxed one, to boot).

Chapter 9 Success Secret #9: Synergy

You don't have to go it alone with your college experience. You can use the energy and resources of all sorts of helpful individuals—your classmates, instructors, librarian, and tutors. You also have access to other support people who are ready and willing to assist you, if you learn to ask. The reason this is a secret is that we actually know a way for you to network in college to make your "effort of one" multiply so that you reap the synergistic "results of many." This chapter shows you how to achieve these results.

Chapter 10   Success Secret #10: Motivation

If you find that you are trying hard with little to show for your efforts, check out this chapter. It takes out the guesswork and reveals what you are doing wrong. There are actually motivation rules, tools, and principles that, when used, will make getting the job done or even just getting started look easy.

Chapter 11   Success Secret #11: Time Management

Time, like money, is a resource you have at your disposal to take you toward your goals and dreams or away from them. We all get the same 24 hours in a day. No more and no less. However, some students use their time so effectively that it seems they have more to spare for things they enjoy. Is it magic? No! They know the secrets of planning their time for better results. The amazing thing is that it is not beyond anyone's reach to mimic what these students are doing to get the same excellent results in time management. Best of all, for all you procrastinators, this chapter shares ways you can turn your procrastination into a success tool!

Chapter 12   Success Secret #12: Stress Management

Without some stress, your life would not have much meaning. The goal is to have the optimum level of stress in which you are effective and productive, and yet healthy and balanced. If there were a way you could learn to increase the threshold of the amount of stress you could gracefully and productively endure, wouldn't you want to know how to do it? This chapter will give you the tools for managing stress.

Appendix   Web Sites, References, and Readings

This is your guide to finding even more details about the success secrets and best practices outlined in this book.

We wish you great success on your journey and want you to know that you are not alone. We—and thousands of other successful students—are cheering you on.

CHAPTER 1

Success Secret #1: Study Skills

"The purpose of studying is learning the material, not just memorizing it."

Anonymous

No matter how much you want to go deep sea diving, you cannot do it successfully if you do not have the right training and tools. The same is true for academic success. You need the right tools for the job. In this chapter, we will take a look at some effective study skills as well as some helpful test-taking strategies to increase your chance of academic success.

The Correct Textbook Tool

To increase your opportunity for success as a student, you need to read the book that has been selected for your class. Pay close attention to the edition of the textbook listed on the syllabus. You may be tempted to purchase a less expensive used textbook, and may accidentally get an earlier edition rather than the required one. Publishers come out with new editions because content has changed or new material has been added. In the new edition, authors may update cases and content to reflect trends and changes in the subjects covered. Students who purchase earlier editions are then surprised to find that the class lecture doesn't match what they have read. They are especially surprised when they turn in an assignment based on a case study in Chapter 2 or answered the questions at the end of the chapter and discover that all their answers are wrong because the case studies and questions are entirely different in the new edition of the book.

This doesn't mean you can't purchase a used book if it is the correct edition. Just make sure the edition of the textbook you purchase is the one being used.

Reading Tools

The following sections present reading tools that can assist you in becoming a more efficient and productive reader. If you use these tools while reading, you will become a much better student, and you will find studying for tests to be less difficult than it was in the past.

Preview Your Material

When you preview material, you focus on titles, headlines, topic sentences, the first sentences in the paragraphs, the introduction, and the conclusion. By reading these items, you should gain a basic understanding of the topic and main ideas.

Practice Pre-Reading Techniques

Pre-reading is using the skimming and scanning techniques to grasp an awareness of the entire passage in a "nutshell." You do not read each word, but you search for the overall structure and content of the material before you actually read for comprehension. By pre-reading, you focus on what is essential and save a great deal of time.

When you are pre-reading, you are seeking the main topic and the general ideas of the material. You are not reading for content specifics. What you need to search for and read are these items:

- Book title

- Chapter titles

- Headings or objectives

- Anything that is italic, bold, highlighted, or in larger print

- Maps, charts, and diagrams

- First and last sentence of each paragraph

- Anything in a box, underlined, or somehow set off for your eyes to catch

- First and last paragraphs and summary of a passage

Skimming

The difference between skimming and scanning in pre-reading is important. When you skim and scan, you do not read every word. You let your eyes move quickly over the sentences and get a feel for what is being said. You can also think ahead about what you are searching for and search for it.

If you want to know where the story takes place, for example, you search for a location or place. You let your eyes move quickly until you come across this information.

Skimming allows you to become familiar with the organization and general content of the material you are going to read. To skim effectively, read the title and section headings. Next, read the titles of any maps, charts, or graphs. Also read the entire introduction. Finally, read the first sentence of each section or paragraph and the last paragraph or summary.

You are skimming for the main idea, asking yourself these questions: Who? What? When? Where? Why? and How? as you read. Doing so puts you in a critical frame of mind and enables you to identify the main points.

Scanning

When you scan, you are searching for specific information within a text without reading the entire text. This involves looking for key words, special typographical features (such as bullets, bold, italic, and so on), or any other features that highlight facts. When you scan material, look for the main idea of the book, chapter, section, and paragraph. You will want to mentally recall the main ideas involved at the end of each section so that you can create your own **mind map.** For more information on mind maps, go to

http://www.jcu.edu.au/studying/services/studyskills/mindmap/howto.html

Review your mind map in intervals: Immediately after you study, again in 24 hours, after one week, and then in one month. If you need more information on how to preview and pre-read by skimming and scanning, enter those words in a search engine on the Internet; you will find more ideas and practice tips.

Find Your Favorite Studying Method

Try out some tried and true approaches that combine previewing and pre-reading for improving your reading skills and retention. One method that students have found particularly helpful is called PQR3. In this method, you Preview what you will learn from the material, Question what you will learn, Read the selection, Recite what you are learning in your own words periodically as you read, and finally Review what you have read when you are finished. Another method is SQRW. This is particularly helpful for reading textbooks. Here, you Survey by thinking about what you already know on the topic, Question what you will learn, Read the selection, and Write the questions and answers in your notebook. For more details on this method, go to this site:

http://www.how-to-study.com/pqr.htm

Using this method, you become familiar with the content, chapter headings, key charts, and diagrams. You repeat this process with each subsequent chapter.

Textbook-Marking Tools

You may have been conditioned to the rule "Do not write in books" from the time you were small until you were out of high school. In college, you hear "Highlight and write in those textbooks." It's okay. You now have permission to write in and highlight your text. Don't be traumatized. It can be quite a "highlighting" experience.

Completely read a chapter before you start marking and highlighting. Be extremely selective. Don't underline or jot down everything. When you put notes in the margins, use your own words. Be brief. Underline meaningful phrases rather than complete sentences. Be quick. You don't have all day for marking. Read, go back for a mini-overview, and make your markings. Then attack the next portion of the chapter. Be neat. Neatness takes conscious effort, but doesn't require additional time. In fact, neatness can save time later because you waste time figuring out what you scribbled or wrote. Organize facts and ideas into categories. Try cross-referencing information, identifying pointers to other places in the same document or to other information sources where you can find related information.

Note-Taking Tools

Taking notes doesn't have to be difficult. Make it easy on yourself. Have two systems: one for taking notes in class and the other for creating notes for reviewing facts you need to learn.

Take Lecture Notes

If you remember these simple note-taking tips, note-taking in your courses can become less challenging. You will find that your success rate will continue to rise.

- **Use a three-ring binder for keeping lecture notes, handouts, and your notes from the textbook and reading.** You are less likely to spend time hunting for important documents if they are all in one place. You can arrange pages with lecture notes and corresponding handouts next to each other. If you miss a lecture, you can easily add the missing notes.

- **Date and number your handouts.**

- **Give yourself extra blank space in your notes and plenty of room to write.**

- **Write your notes in pen and use only one side of your paper.** Doing so will make them easier to read.

- **Use paper that has a wide margin on the left side.** If you can't find paper with a wide margin, draw it.

- **Write your notes on the right side of the margin line.** You can then use the left margin when reviewing your notes.

- **Take as many notes as you can.**

- **If you miss something, leave a space.** You can fill it in later. Do not stop taking notes if you become lost or confused. Add a question mark, and leave a space; you can come back to what you missed later.

- **Use abbreviations** (presented in the section on additional note-taking tools).

- **Work with your notes as soon as you can after class.** You can organize them and make them clearer while they are still fresh in your mind.

- **As you review your notes, look at the information as answers to questions.** As these questions become clear to you, jot them, as well as key words, in the left margin. Then you can recall the information by covering up the right side of your notes and testing yourself.

Use Note Cards

Creating and using note cards can alleviate anxiety about remembering facts and can be a valuable portable study tool. Note cards are great for learning terminology and also to present written information out of sequence. Use these tips for working with note cards:

- **On a 3x5 card, write the term or question you need to memorize.** On the other side of the card, write the definition, description, or answer.

- **Start compiling cards at the beginning of the quarter or semester.**

- **Carry the cards with you and review them often**—while standing in line, waiting for an appointment, waiting for a ride, and so on.

Repetition is the best way to learn some material. Note cards let you readily review the information time and again.

Additional Note-Taking Tools

Learn to use even more note-taking tools—tools that let you take more notes in less time. Our first tool is that you free yourself of worries about punctuation. Taking time to decide what punctuation you need and then write it is unnecessary. The following table lists other common tools to use while taking notes.

Note-Taking Tools

Use Common Symbols and Graphics

=	equal	?	does not equal	
*	important	**	very important	
>	greater than	<	less than	
w/	with	w/o	without	
&	and	#	number	
$	cost, money	( ),{ },[ ]	information that belongs together	

Use Common Abbreviations

cf	compare	eg	for example	dept	department
mx	maximum	mn	minimum	vs	versus
NYC	New York City				

Use First Syllable of a Word

bus	business	pol	policy	lib	liberal

Eliminate Final Letters; Use Just Enough to Recognize the Abbreviation

intro	introduction	info	information	assoc	association

Use Apostrophes to Abbreviate Words

gov't	government	cont'd	continued

Omit Vowels from the Middle of Words

bkgrd	background	estmt	estimate	rdng	reading

Many students have a fear of forgetting what the tools mean. After you get into the habit of using them, you won't forget.

Study Tools

The following Web site has a variety of study tools designed to make you a more effective and efficient learner.

http://www.studygs.net

The sections that follow explain the study tools referred to as chunking and MURDER, as well as several other tools.

Chunking

You can use chunking as a study tool. With chunking, you make a picture of what you are learning. Chunking is effective because people remember pictures more easily than words. You can find out more about chunking and diagrams at the following Web site.

http://www.dushkin.com/connectext/psy/ch07/chunking.mhtml

Another visual aid for chunking is to develop an effective memory by getting a deep and vivid mental picture or impression of what you want to remember and then imagining it.

If you are a visual learner, chunking could be an especially effective tool for you. An assignment in Chapter 3 is to take a learning assessment to determine your learning style. The goal of an assessment is to know yourself well enough to recognize your study strengths and weaknesses.

MURDER

Students seem to have an affinity for the MURDER approach to improving study skills. MURDER stands for:

M = Mood. Be in the correct mood for studying.

U = Understand. Understand what you are learning or highlight it so you can learn it better later.

R = Recall. Recall the information in the section you are studying before you move on.

D = Digest. Integrate what you have learned.

E = Expand. Expand the knowledge you have gained.

R = Review. Review what you have studied.

The following Internet sites are well worth visiting to learn more about the MURDER technique of studying:

http://www.studygs.net/murder.htm

http://www.studyguidezone.com/murderstudysystem.htm

Mnemonic Devices

Mnemonic devices are aids for improving one's memory. These devices can be great for memorizing information. They generally attach new information to be learned to old information already mastered, or to catchwords or phrases that are easily remembered. Following is an example of a mnemonic device.

Example of a Mnemonic Device

For chemistry class, you need to memorize these seven diatomic molecules:

1. bromine
2. hydrogen
3. chlorine
4. fluorine
5. oxygen
6. nitrogen
7. iodine

To create a catchphrase for this list, begin by underlining the first letter of each molecule. Then make up a phrase, such as "Brian helps Claire find out new ideas."

The following sections present three other mnemonic devices: jingles, acronyms, and acrostics. If you review these helpful tools often, they can help you become a success in class.

Jingles

Jingles are rhyming phrases sometimes put to song. Many people have used a common jingle to memorize the number of days in each month. You can use this jingle for accounting and business math concepts when you need to remember how many days are in a month in calculating discounts on notes and interest.

Example of a Jingle

Thirty days has September,

April, June, and November.

All the rest have 31,

except February, which has 28;

Leap year, 29.

Memorize that jingle, and you will remember the number of days in each month forever. Make up jingles for other things you need to memorize.

Acronyms

Acronyms are catchwords. For example, HOMES is the catchword for learning the Great Lakes—Huron, Ontario, Michigan, Erie, and Superior. To create an acronym, write the information you need to remember in a list, number the list, and then underline the first letter in each word to see whether you have a recognizable catchword. CANU, for example, is the catchword for naming the only spot in the U.S. where four states meet: Colorado, Arizona, New Mexico, and Utah. Following is another example.

Example of an Acronym

In your psychology course, you must name the four symptoms of schizophrenia. Begin by making a list of the symptoms.

1. withdrawal

2. hallucinations

3. inappropriate emotional response

4. delusions

When you underline the first letter of each symptom, you get the catchword *whid*. Whid is easy to say, easy to remember, and will trigger the names of the four symptoms when you think of it.

Using a silly acronym can help you to remember your catchword and the information attached to it. The important thing is it helps you to become a better student.

Acrostics

Acrostics are catch phrases. The steps for developing acronyms and acrostics are the same. If you need to memorize the colors of the spectrum, for example, you can remember the name Roy G. Biv. Red, orange, yellow, green, blue, indigo, and violet are the colors of the spectrum.

Basic Online Class Study Skills

The study skills you need if you are an online student are the same as those stated throughout this chapter. You may not have to do a lot of note-taking, but the skills will come in handy anyway. If you need to bone up on your math or writing skills, do so. Trust us. Your keyboarding skills will improve as you go online for your classes. If you are a slow

(continued)

(continued)

keyboarder, you can practice this or take a class, but you will also improve as you go. You can also check out a typing book from your local or school library and practice your typing skills.

Hundreds of successful online students have identified certain tools you can use to improve your ability to handle anything that comes your way in the online environment.

• Of greatest importance are the computer and Internet connection. This may seem basic, but without them, you have no class! Check your school to find the minimum hardware requirements. However, successful online students have nearly unanimously commented that you should not skimp on technology. The extra money you spend up front on faster hardware and Internet technology will be recouped in short order with substantial savings of time.

Know what equipment will be needed and that you have access to this equipment on a regular basis. If you are behind a firewall, such as on a military base, make sure your IT people grant you access to the URL address for your class. Make sure your Internet connection is working before the class starts, and know the Internet browser and the setting for it to take your course. If you have a program that disables "pop-ups" on your computer, you may want to enable pop-ups. Some course platforms need the pop-up function for you to send mail in class. You may want to ask your school about this issue.

• Although you don't need to be a computer wizard, you will want to have or be willing to learn basic computer skills so that the process is less frustrating. Do not let the lack of computer skills deter you, however, as many successful online students could only send e-mail when they enrolled. Your willingness to learn will be the key to your success. Hitting a learning curve can be frustrating or even daunting at times, but your willingness to try quieting your mind and allowing the new thoughts to come in can take you far. Asking for help and calling the tech support hotline will get you ahead of the game as well.

- You will still need to get a textbook and other required material. Do not overlook this point and think you can get away without required materials. Get the textbook and get it early. We cannot tell you how many students we have watched drop their online classes costing them dearly because they waited too long to buy the textbook. Somehow they thought that it would be okay if they did not have the textbook, that somehow their teacher would give them an extension. Wrong.

  In fact, many online platforms do not even allow instructors to accept late assignments or quizzes. When the week is closed, you can view it, but you cannot deposit assignments or add to discussions. So get your books early.

  This also applies to any software you may need to get for your course. Get what is required and get it soon. The more time you have to familiarize yourself with the intricacies of software such as word processing programs and spreadsheets, the better. The last thing you want is to fail before you have a chance to succeed. So get your basic tools ready and use your books and supplement material as intended.

  Preview the material before you go online. Do all optional assignments to make your online time more effective. This is being fiercely responsible for yourself.

- Take the time to click on illustrations, examples, definitions, and other links. This way you enrich your understanding and solidify what you are learning.

  Be curious about your online class and explore it. Try new computer commands in the course to fully learn how to navigate. You can learn a great deal about your course structure by punching buttons and seeing where they lead you.

Study Skills Conclusion

The tools of getting the correct textbook, improving your reading and learning skills, and making certain that you have effective technological equipment are all recognized as extremely important by successful students and teachers alike. There really is no excuse for any student to do anything but succeed in an on-campus or online environment with this information. Becoming a successful student just takes a little elbow grease, and we guarantee it will pay off.

Best Practices Summary
Do's and Don'ts of Success Secret #1
Study Skills

Do

- Do always buy your textbooks in advance. If you are an online student, remember that sometimes your reading assignments will be in the condensed format, that is they will be summarized and the entire reading assignment will not be shown. Whether you are onsite or online, it's to your benefit to get a head start.

- Do brush up on your reading and summarizing skills. Doing so pays off in time-savings and better grades every time.

- Do take time to work on your learning skills. The transition from teacher-centered learning (in which the focus is on the teacher) to learner-centered learning (focusing on the learner) is important. Don't overlook it.

- Do get the best computer hardware and software, especially if you are an online student. If you don't, you probably have a long and tough road ahead of you. It is better to spend a few extra dollars than be sorry.

- Do have a reliable and high-speed (if available) Internet service, a time-saving feature that pays for itself day after day.

Don't

- Don't wait until the last minute to buy your textbook.

- Don't underestimate your ability to learn. Tools will help you finish the job successfully.

- Don't use absolutes of "can't," "won't," or "never." You can and will if you simply try. Repeat this statement often: "I can do this."

Success Secret #1 Assignment 1: Search the Web for Study Skills Topics

In this assignment, you search the Web for additional information about improving your studying skills.

1. Visit at least three of the following Web addresses from this chapter (or choose other URLs from the Study Skills section in the back of the book, *More Useful Tips*):

   http://www.how-to-study.com/pqr.htm

   http://www.jcu.edu.au/studying/services/studyskills/mindmap/howto.html

   http://www.studygs.net

   http://www.dushkin.com/connectext/psy/ch07/chunking.mhtml

   http://www.studyguidezone.com/resources_tips.htm

2. Find six study skills that interest you.

3. In a word processing document that you can share with your class, give a brief description of your thoughts on each of these topics.

   List the URLs you selected and your six tips.

(continued)

(continued)

Explain why you feel the way you do.

Include the reason you found the tips helpful and whether you plan to use them.

Success Secret #1 Assignment 2: Practice Study Skills

In this assignment, you practice some of the study skills you have learned. Choose one of your classes in which you are challenged. Apply the study skills to that class from now until you take your first exam in that class. You should do the following:

1. Read the chapters or units before they are discussed in class.

2. Practice the skimming and scanning reading tips.

3. Review the note-taking tips that you read in this chapter.

4. Jot down notes while you read.

5. Jot down questions you have about the information you read.

6. When you get to class, focus on some of the objectives that were listed in the beginning of the chapter. Listen for key terms. Now is the time to use your note-taking skills. Practice taking notes each class period before the exam.

7. When the instructor asks for questions during or at the end of the lecture, ask those questions you jotted down earlier.

8. Find out when the first exam will be and what type of exam will be given.

(continued)

(continued)

9.   Read over the chapter for the second time, focusing on the lecture notes, terms, and ideas the instructor stressed.

CHAPTER 2

Success Secret #2: Test-Taking Skills

"There's no such thing as a stupid question, but they're the easiest to answer."

Tech Support Guy at www.techsupportguy.com

Test-taking can be scary. However, tests are something you can't get away from. For you to earn your degree, the school has to have some way of knowing you understand the material in your classes. Your instructors have to test you to see whether you learned anything.

Test-Preparation Tools

Successful students start preparing for exams on the first day of class. You can do this by reading the syllabus. You need to know how many exams you have, their point values, and when they will take place. Some exams are timed; if the allotted time is not obvious, you will want to ask your instructor how much time is allotted for each exam. Also ask if your exams are open book. You will want to transfer the exam dates into your own personal palm-pilot/day timer or calendar. Then you will be thinking of your exams and reviewing for them throughout the entire course rather than just one exam at a time.

Review for several short bursts rather than one long period. Your review is much more than just rereading the lecture notes and the assignments. Listen for hints from your instructor. If the instructor says, "You should know the following information," or if the instructor repeats something more than once, you can be assured you probably will see it again in an exam. If the instructor reviews for an exam on a certain day, make sure you are there. If you miss class during the review, get the review notes from a classmate.

Get together with students in your class and form a study group. These reviews can reinforce your learning. If you cannot be part of a study group, at least have a buddy available to call or e-mail if you are stuck. Don't forget that you can contact your instructor as well. The more people you have to support you and help you, the better.

Try to predict what will be asked on the exam, and then outline your responses. Don't be afraid to ask your instructor whether certain material will be on the exam.

Depending on the course material, you may want to use old-fashioned flashcards. It has been reported that you must hear or see something about eight times to learn and remember it. That is the beauty of flashcards. You will be relearning the material simply by making the flashcards and then reviewing them.

Specific Test-Taking Strategies

Listed below are some great test-taking strategies for specific types of exams. You will be surprised how much better you will do on tests if you review these tools several times over the quarter or semester. Remember, the more you see or hear something, the more you will remember it. If you really pay attention to these tools, we know you can increase your grade by 10 points or more.

True/False Exam Tools

Following are tools you can use when your exam has true/false questions.

- **Determine the number of questions and budget your time.** Usually, an exam that contains true/false questions has many of them. If so, answer each question quickly. It may not be worth a lot of time to get one question right if it is worth only two points on a 100-point test.

- **Read each question carefully.** Remember that if any part of a statement is false, the entire statement is false. Most questions contain a combination of who, what, when, or how facts. If any of these facts are wrong, the statement is false.

- **Look for qualifiers.** Words such as never, all, none, and always generally indicate a statement is false. Words and phrases such as on the other hand, sometimes, generally, often, frequently, and mostly indicate a statement is true.

- **Answer the questions you know first.** Often answers to questions you don't know are supplied in other questions. Go back and answer difficult questions last.

- **When guessing, do not change answers.** Research indicates your first answer is usually right. However, don't be afraid to change answers when you have good reason to do so.

- **"Reason" statements tend to be false.** When something is given as the "reason" or "cause" or "because of" something else, the statement tends to be false.

- **Answer all questions.** Unless points are deducted for incorrect responses, leave enough time to answer all questions. Mark all remaining or unanswered questions as true; in a true/false exam, a slight majority of the answers are usually true.

Multiple-Choice Exam Tools

Following are tools you can use when your exam has multiple-choice questions.

- **Attempt to answer the question without looking at the options.**

- **If necessary, cover the answers with your hand.**

- **Eliminate the distracters, those answers that you know are obviously wrong. Cross those out.**

- **Analyze the options as true/false questions.** In a negatively worded question (for example, which of the following are not), put a T or F beside each option, and then select the false statement.

- Never be afraid to use common sense in determining answers.

- It is sometimes easy to confuse yourself by attempting to recall the right answer rather than simply reasoning through the question. Make sure your answer makes sense.

- Answer the questions you know first.

- Often answers to questions you don't know are supplied in other questions. Go back to answer the difficult questions later.

- When guessing, do not change answers.

- Research indicates your first answer is usually best. However, don't be afraid to change answers when you have a good reason for doing so.

- When guessing, choose answers that are not the first or last option.

- Research indicates that the option in the middle with the most words is usually the correct response.

- If the first option is a correct one, look at the last option to make sure it is not an "all of the above" option. The same is true for "none of the above" questions.

- Answer all the questions.

- Unless points are deducted for incorrect responses, leave enough time to answer all the questions.

- Allow time at the end to check answers and for carelessness.

Short-Answer or Fill-in-the-Blank Exam Questions

There are few if any "tricks" for short-answer or fill-in-the-blank exam questions.

- It is best to over-study.

- Answer the questions you know first.

- **Note the time you have to complete the exam and then give yourself a specific number of minutes per question.** When you do not know the answer to a question, skip it and come back to it later. Just remember: Make sure to look over your exam when you are finished in case you forget to answer some questions.

- **When you prepare for the exam, focus on facts and key words.**

- **Look over your materials as though you were going to write the exam.**

- **Try to predict questions that would be found on this type of exam.**

Matching Questions

Following are tools you can use when your exam has matching questions.

- **Determine the pattern of the matching questions.**

- **Take a minute before you begin answering questions to determine exactly what is being matched.** Are you matching people with quotes, words with definitions, or events with descriptions?

- **Choose the longest column to read first.**

- **One column will probably have more information than the other column.** If you begin by reading the column with the most information, matching it to the column with the least amount of reading, you can avoid having to reread the lengthy material.

- **Answer the questions you know first.**

- **If you aren't sure about one of the matching items, come back and match it up later.** You may find you have only a match or two left at the end and you can make a decision then. Once again, don't forget to double-check your exam when you are finished to make sure you didn't leave something unmarked or unanswered.

- **With each answer, cross out items used from both columns.** This timesaver lets you know you have already matched items; you don't have to waste time rereading over and over those items you have already matched.

Essay Exam Tools

Essay exams can be fairly easy if you follow the tips in this section. It has several pointers on how to write a successful essay exam. Review these tips often so you become very familiar with them.

For essay questions, we advise you to read the question carefully, brainstorm for creative ideas, and then use them to make an outline before you begin writing. Brainstorm and outline even if the essay test is timed; doing so will make the process easier and quicker in the long run. Learn to allow your first ideas to flow and know you can edit them into a more formal essay later. Do not write for the reader (your instructor) while you are in the creative stage. The more logical your outline, the easier your essay is to follow and the more likely you are to get a better score. Typically essays are written in the third person unless you are talking about yourself or telling someone what to do. The next section gives our step-by-step plan for answering an essay question.

A Step-by-Step Approach to Answering Essay Questions

Get into the habit of approaching essay questions in a step-by-step fashion. Here are the steps you can follow:

1. **Read the question carefully.**

   Think: Does it ask for your opinion?

2. **Brainstorm ideas or create a mind web, also referred to as a mind map.** A mind web is a way of graphically organizing your thoughts.

3. **Categorize your topic, numbering each category.**

   Think: There's an obvious outline for this topic. What is it?

   I.

   II.

   III.

4. **Rank and sort your brainstormed ideas into your outline.**

   Think: I should have three points of interest (or examples) for each category.

I.

    A.

    B.

    C.

II.

    A.

    B.

    C.

III.

    A.

    B.

    C.

5. **Take a few minutes to rethink the topic from an interesting angle.**

6. **Make sure that your Introduction accomplishes these tasks:**

   - Begin with an attention getter.

   - Have a segue into your topic.

   - Tell the reader your topic.

   - Tell the reader your outline or the categories that you are going to write about.

   - Include a thesis (position) statement.

7. **Begin writing the body of the paper.**

   Think: What phrases can transition smoothly from topic to topic?

   Transition phrase examples:

   Sample Essay Question: Supporters of technology say that it solves problems and leads to a higher quality of life. Opponents argue that technology creates new problems that may threaten or harm the quality of life. Using these two examples, discuss these two positions. Which view of technology do you support? Why?

Transition (phrase) sentence for Paragraph 2:

"To begin with, advances in technology have provided many benefits for mankind. For example, …"

Transition (phrase) sentence for Paragraph 3:

"Although technology has created such advances for modern man, it has also caused many problems and comes at a price to society. An example of how technology can be a detriment is …"

Transition sentence for Paragraph 4:

"As has been discussed, technology has positive and negative aspects. After weighing these differences, I tend to support (USE this word, it came from question) the position that technology, when used responsibly, is far better than living without it. One of the reasons I feel this way is because …"

Conclusion:

"In summary, it has been said that nothing in life comes without a price. In the case of technology, this rule also holds true. The price of advanced technology is a tradeoff for the environment, forced community involvement, and sometimes "playing God" in medical advances. This essay has discussed the two positions of technology. There are no easy answers to the gap created by technology. However, I do believe we can continue to become both technologically advanced and ethically responsible without having these options be mutually exclusive…"

8. **Proofread your answer before submitting it.**

   If you have access to Spell and/or Grammar Check, use them. If they are not available in the online platform, write your essay in Microsoft Word or even an e-mail and spell check it before you copy and paste it into your essay answer box. Proofreading is important. Even simple things such as the number of spaces after periods and using the proper font and line spacing can improve your overall grade.

Additional Essay Exam Tools

Following are other tools that can help you with essay exams.

- **Memorize key phrases, definitions, or short passages.**

- **Learn main ideas, key terms, steps, and processes.**

- **Know the concepts and ideas, not just names and dates.**

- **Anticipate exam questions.** If you have studied different management styles, for example, you would want to be able to compare and contrast those styles.

- **Read through the entire exam once before you start writing.**

- **If answers come to mind immediately for some questions, jot down key words while they are fresh in your mind, but don't start writing until you have read through the exam once.**

- **Budget your time.** Allow enough time at the end to go back and finish incomplete answers and to proofread your paper.

- **Answer questions you know first.**

- **Don't panic about any question you think you do not know.** Stay calm. Come back to those. As you relax, you probably will remember the answers to those questions later. Come back and do them last.

- **Take time to structure your answer.** Whenever you can, work from a brief outline jotted down on scratch paper before you begin to write. Select what is clearly relevant; try to avoid rambling and repetition.

- **Get to the point.** Make your first sentence sum up your main point. If you are writing a lengthy answer, summarize, in an introductory paragraph, the key points you intend to make. If you aren't sure about something, it is better to have less content and get the facts straight instead of trying to get several sentences together and repeating the same thing over and over. Professors know all the tricks. You can't trick them into thinking you know the information when you don't.

- **Qualify answers when in doubt.** It is better to say "toward the end of the 20th century" than to say "1990" when you can't remember whether it is 1990 or 1992. The general date may be all that is necessary, but you may lose credit for a specific but incorrect date.

- **Take time at the end to reread the exam.** Make sure you have answered all the questions and have answered all parts of the question.

Words in Essay Exams

This section introduces words that are commonly used in essay exams. Become familiar with these words and what is expected from you when you are completing the essay exam. Being familiar with the words can make the difference between receiving partial credit and no credit on an answer. If an exam asks you to discuss something and you make a list, for example, you will lose points and could possibly get zero points for your answer. Professors are very serious about the wording of essay questions and how they should be answered.

Common Words Used in Essay Exams

Compare	Examine characteristics in order to determine likeness.
Contrast	Stress dissimilarities, differences, or unlikeness of association.
Criticize	Express your judgment with respect to the correctness or merit of the factors under consideration.
Define	Write concise, clear, authoritative meanings. Keep in mind the class to which the item belongs and whatever differentiated it from all other classes.

Discuss	Examine, analyze carefully. Present pros and cons.
Enumerate	A list or outline form of reply–recount, one by one, the points required.
Evaluate	Present an appraisal, stressing advantages and limitations.
Explain	Clarify and interpret the material you present.
Illustrate	Present a figure, diagram, or concrete example.
Interpret	Translate, solve, or comment on the subject. Give a judgment or reaction.
Justify	Prove your thesis or show grounds for your decision.
List	Present an itemized series or tabulation.
Outline	Give main points and supplementary material in a systematic manner.
Prove	Establish something with certainty by citing evidence or by logical reasoning.
Relate	Emphasize connections and associations.
Review	Emphasize and comment briefly in organized sequence on the major points.
State	Express the main points in a brief, clear way.
Summarize	Give in condensed form the main points or facts.
Trace	Give a description of progress, sequence, or development from the point of origin.

Test-Anxiety Tools

If you have test anxiety, you don't have to be defeated. You can take action. First, let's discuss how you can recognize test anxiety. Some students actually get physical distress symptoms such as nausea, headaches, faintness, or feeling overheated or too cold. Other students feel less physical symptoms, but more emotional ones. They want to or even do cry; laugh too much; or feel helpless, angry, or frustrated. Either way, test tension affects their performance. The students often stop breathing or have panic attacks or hyperventilate. Some students become so tense in the neck and shoulders that they can't get enough blood to their brain, affecting their ability to think well and causing them to blank out or have racing thoughts that are hard to slow down and focus. Most students have some level of stress around an exam but can manage it effectively. If you suffer from major test anxiety, fear not. There is hope. Begin by taking slow, deep breaths.

Prepare Physically

Being well prepared for an exam is very important to reduce your stress level. Use the test-taking tools discussed in Chapter 1. Stay healthy by eating nutritious food, exercising, and getting enough sleep. Yes, we know you have heard it all before. The truth is that your body fuels your brain and must be in good shape for mental trials.

Prepare by making sure you have all your supplies with you for the exam. It always amazes professors how many students show up on exam day with no test-taking implements in hand. Don't be one of the students who show up for an exam without a pen or pencil. If you need to use a calculator for a math, accounting, or other course, make sure that you take it with you, it works, and the batteries are new. It is always a good idea to bring a spare calculator with you just in case yours breaks down. Have a snack handy and some water.

Lessen your stress by knowing when and where your exam is. Many schools have different times set aside for final exams. Double-check the date, time, and place of your exam so that you aren't anxiously hunting for that information on test day.

Prepare Mentally

Thoughts are exercise for your brain. What you think about will expand. If you are living in fear of the exam, it will start consuming you, literally running your life. Rather, use positive thought patterns and messages. Your thoughts will eventually create your beliefs, which will in turn result in actions. Change your thoughts, and soon you will start affecting your reactions. Say these affirmations to yourself:

"Of course I can do well on this test."

"I studied, and the answers will come to me."

"I am a confident test-taker."

Repeat these simple affirmations daily until test day. If you happen to freeze up, breathe. And keep doing deep, slow breathing.

You can teach yourself to calm down by repeating a calming word, such as "Peace," while you are taking the exam. This word can work as a trigger for your mind. You can take some deep, slow breaths and keep saying the trigger word throughout the exam. If needed, stop, stretch, breathe, and say, "I will do fine. I know this material. I will do well." Then go back to your test.

You have learned the habit of being stressed for an exam, and it will take a bit of undoing to get a new habit around test taking, but you can! That is the good news. You are not the first one to have text anxiety. Others have moved to a new place beyond it, and so can you! The ability to do the same is in you. Believe in yourself and stop comparing your insides to other's outsides. Stay positive and be well prepared. If you feel that your test anxiety is unmanageable, consider working with someone who does energy work (such as Reiki) around panic.

For those with substantial test anxiety, we recommend the following test anxiety tools.

Overcome Test Anxiety

Follow this checklist to overcome test anxiety:

- ❑ The key to the process of successful test-taking lies in time management: Know in advance when the tests and quizzes are and how much they are weighted toward your total points for the course.

- ❑ From the beginning of the course, ask about the midterm and final exams so you can plan for them. (If an exam is an online test, find out whether you have unlimited time or it is timed. Often online courses will turn on and off at specific times. Find out what time zone the test refers to and the dates. Put this information in your calendar.) Often it helps to work backward from assignments. Work back from the due date.

- ❑ Find out what format the test is in: essay, true/false, multiple choice, and so on.

- ❑ Be present for the midterm and final reviews if they are available. Your presence is essential to understand what is most likely going to be tested.

❑ Study in the way that is successful for you. If cramming is successful and you enjoy it, then cram. If cramming works against you, form different study habits.

❑ If cramming does not work for you (and it does not work for many students, although they continue to use it anyway), study 15 to 30 minutes a day instead of three hours the night before.

❑ Guess what the instructor might test you on and ask for test study tips. Most instructors will give them to you.

❑ Commit important concepts to memory.

❑ Eat before the test—something with protein to sustain you, but not a lot of carbs. They will give you a quick sugar rush but then make you sleepy.

❑ Prepare mentally to take the test by breathing deeply and visualizing a positive outcome, a perfect grade.

❑ Along with breathing, think of something that relaxes you before you take the test and the sweet victory you will feel after you ace it!

❑ Give your brain at least one hour to rest before the exam.

❑ Read the directions on the test twice before beginning.

❑ Read all the questions on the test before you start. This allows your subconscious to start solving some questions as you are working on others.

❑ Use the process of elimination. If you do not know the correct answer on a multiple-choice question, try to figure it out by crossing out the answers that you are certain are wrong.

❑ If you are not sure, guess. Statistically speaking, random guessing won't hurt you.

❑ Do not cross out any answers in a test unless you are certain they are wrong.

❑ If you get stuck on a question, make a note in the margin and move on, letting your subconscious work on the problem you are stuck on.

❑ Go at your own pace.

❑ Eliminate negative self-statements.

❑ Use humor in taking tests. This reduces anxiety and can improve your performance.

❑ If you have a brain freeze, stop, take a deep breath, and count to 10. Tell yourself you know the answers, and they are coming to you easily. Keep breathing. Then go to the next question.

❑ Realize that you know what you know and keep moving forward.

❑ Give yourself a reward when the test is over.

❑ Use the test results to study for future tests.

❑ Go back and figure out why you got an answer wrong. Question your instructor if you don't understand why you got it wrong. Explain your logic; you might get more points by doing so.

We know you are thinking that those things were already discussed. Remember this: If you see something more than once, you have a better chance of remembering it.

Test-Taking Skills Conclusion

Students suffer from test-taking anxiety for a variety of reasons. The main reason is not being well prepared for an exam. Other reasons students suffer from test anxiety are worries they have about past performance, how well others are doing, and the negative consequences they face if they fail. If you read over this chapter and use the tools we have given you, that should alleviate most or all of your test anxiety, especially anxiety concerning being well prepared. You will alleviate other anxieties by continuing to build your self-confidence when you read the chapters on attitude and motivation that are coming up.

Best Practices Summary
Do's and Don'ts of Success Secret #2
Test-Taking Skills

Do

- Do use the study skills you learned in Chapter 1.

- Do listen in class for hints about what might be on exam.

- Do study for your exam.

- Do learn the tools for the different types of tests given.

- Do practice test-taking skills. Develop templates for answering essay-type questions in an outline format.

- Do pay close attention to and know what the words mean that are being used in essay questions. (Examples: discuss and list.)

- Do learn how to overcome test anxiety. It will help your test performance and overall grade. It is advisable to develop templates for answering essay-type questions in an outline format.

- Do learn how to overcome test anxiety. It will help your test performance and overall grade.

Don't

- Don't study at the last minute, trying to cram for exams. Your body and mind need rest and care if they are to function well.

- Don't worry about how others are doing, your past performance, or negative thoughts on "what if I fail."

- Don't let test anxiety rule you. Test taking is a learned skill. The more confident you become in your skill, the less anxiety you will have.

Success Secret #2 Assignment 1: Learn About Test Anxiety

In this assignment, you explore a Web site to learn more about test anxiety.

1. Go to the following Web site:

   http://ub-counseling.buffalo.edu/stresstestanxiety

2. Answer the following three questions.

   What are six physical symptoms of test anxiety?

   What are the effects of test anxiety?

   What are five things you can do to reduce test anxiety?

Success Secret #2 Assignment 2: Practice Test-Taking Skills

In this assignment, implement the suggestions in this chapter.

1. Find out the format of the test and what might be on the exam.

2. Read over the test-taking tips for that format.

3. Take notes if the professor has a test review. Tape the test review if possible.

4. Review the chapters you have read and your notes. Pay special attention to the items gone over during the test review.

5. Get some rest the night before the test. Eat breakfast. Show up early for the exam. Review your notes. Do some relaxation exercises before the exam.

6. Relax and remember that you are well prepared and should do well on your exam.

7. When you receive the results of your exam, note how much better you did compared to what you have done on previous exams.

CHAPTER 3

Success Secret #3: Perception, Learning Styles, and Personality

"Preconceived notions are the locks on the door to wisdom."

Merry Browne

We all go through life being told how we are and why we do the things we do. These preconceived ideas can keep any of us from being successful. In this chapter, you will identify your learning style and personality type. You also will come to understand how knowing yourself better and getting rid of some of those preconceived notions you have about yourself can help you on your road to success.

Perception

You may not know it, but the perception you have of yourself affects your success. This perception (how you see yourself) comes from conditioning throughout your life. You learn "how you are" (that is, that you are not good at math or that you are clumsy) from parents, family, friends, teachers, and acquaintances. After the perception of "how you are" is firmly in your subconscious, it stays there until the perception is changed. Your perception and self-concept can sabotage your success.

In this chapter, we look at how identifying your learning style and personality type can change how you see yourself. This Secret also shows you how not knowing these two things can affect your academic success.

As was stated previously, the perception you have of "how you are" is the result of conditioning, from statements you have heard over and over again. For example, you may have heard that you are not good at math. Your parents have told you, teachers have told you, your spouse may have told you, and you may have told yourself. You have been told that you're not good at math so many times you finally believe it.

People act not in accordance with the truth, but with what they believe the truth to be. What if the reason for your not doing well in math is that your teacher used a teaching style that was not effective with your learning style? What if you had no idea you even had a learning style and were studying in the wrong way? The question then becomes this: Is it that you're not good at math or that you have never used your learning style properly to process mathematical information?

Learning Styles

A learning style can be defined as how you take in information, process it, and learn it. To better understand what your learning style is, you will want to take a learning style assessment, sometimes referred to as an inventory.

Don't let the word *assessment* scare you. It isn't a test or an exam. It is just a tool used to find out information about you. Many people find the accuracy of assessments amazing.

To find out more about your learning style, complete Assignment 1 in this chapter and then read the sections on the three basic learning styles—visual, auditory, and kinesthetic/tactile—and study tips for each learning style. Knowing your learning style may give you a slightly different perception of yourself.

When you are taking the assessment, you should

- **Read each statement carefully.**

- **Choose the statement that comes closest to stating how you are *most* of the time.** We can't state enough that you need to mark the statement that comes closest to how you act and behave most of the time. If you just mark items without thinking about them, the results will not be valid. A student once took the assessment, marking everything the opposite of the truth. The results showed that this person was extremely outgoing. In reality, he was extremely shy and quiet. He was called on in class many times because the instructor knew that he was more outgoing than others. The student was very uncomfortable and finally confessed that he had cheated on the assessment. He was glad to get back into his comfort zone. Take your time, read the statements carefully, and answer honestly so that your results will be more accurate.

- **If you do not understand a word, look it up in the dictionary.** Misunderstanding the meaning of a word can make a difference in the results of the assessment. People will not think you are stupid if you look up words. They probably will be relieved to see someone else doesn't know a word, and they will not feel bad about using a dictionary. Be a leader; don't follow the herd.

Remember this general rule when looking at your test results: These results will not match you exactly. The test is only a tool to give you a clearer picture of yourself. However, if you answered the questions honestly, you probably will be surprised at how accurate the results are. You might even change some self-perceptions that have been holding you back.

Success Secret #3 Assignment 1: Find Your Learning Style

In this assignment, you complete a short, easy learning style assessment. It can give you a basic awareness of your learning style.

1. Go to this Web site:

   http://www.metamath.com/lsweb/dvclearn.htm

(continued)

(continued)

2. Click on Learning Styles Survey to begin the learning styles inventory.

3. For accurate results, answer the questions honestly and "like you are most of the time."

4. Save and print your results to share with the class.

Visual Learners

If your highest number scored is for visual learning, you are considered to be a visual learner. According to *Webster's Dictionary,* the learning style definition of "visual" is this:

> "Of, relating to, or employing visual aids, attained or maintained by sight, and producing mental images."

Approximately 40 percent of learners are visual learners, who learn best by seeing and picturing. Pictures, videos, diagrams, and demonstrations are excellent ways for a visual learner to learn new material. A visual learner prefers to read, to look up and see written or drawn information, to be given written instructions.

If you are a visual learner, you probably

- Make vivid and detailed movies in your mind about what you are reading.

- Pay close attention to the body language and facial expressions of others.

- Are well organized and neat.

- Have a keen awareness of your environment and use image and color to increase retention of information.

If you are a visual learner, you will want to use these study tips:

- **Look for videos to supplement the subject you are learning.**

- **Spend time looking at the diagrams and examples.**

- **Read your text before you go to class.**

- **Take notes in different color ink and highlight your books with different colors.**

- **Highlight and underline key terms and concepts.**

- **Look up words you do not understand.**

- **Buy an inexpensive dictionary and keep it with you.**

Auditory Learners

If your higher score is in the auditory section, you are an auditory learner. The definition of "auditory" in this context is this:

"Of, relating to, or experienced through hearing."

In other words, you learn best by listening. Approximately 30 percent of learners are auditory. An auditory learner prefers lectures and understands verbal directions well.

If you are an auditory learner, you probably

- Learn well through verbal explanations.

- Enjoy class discussion and taking part or watching role-playing.

- Are distracted by noise easily but tend to remember information when associated with sounds.

- Need more time to process information and to ask questions.

- Talk through problems.

- Learn by listening, repeating, and planning aloud.

If you are an auditory learner, you will want to use these study tips:

- **Tape class lectures and test reviews as a helpful study aid.**

- **Start a study group and listen carefully to others who attend the study group session.**

- **Review information by listening to audiotapes, and then repeating the information you need to know.**

Kinesthetic/Tactile Learners

If you scored highest in the kinesthetic/tactile area, you are in the group that makes up approximately 15 percent of all learners. Kinesthetic means

> "Sense mediated by end organs located in muscles, tendons, and joints and stimulated by bodily movements and tensions; also: sensory experience derived from this sense."

The meaning for tactile is this:

> "Perceptible by touch and of or relating to the sense of touch."

Put simply, kinesthetic/tactile learners learn best by doing. Hands-on experience and physical activity are the best methods to use with this type of learner. These learners like to be physically involved in the learning environment.

If you are a kinesthetic/tactile learner, you probably

- Learn well in a lab setting. For example, you learn computer skills best by actually using the computer.

- Learn concepts by applying them.

- Like to do group projects.

- Will try to put something together without reading directions.

- Have trouble sitting still for long periods.

If you are a kinesthetic/tactile learner, you will want to use these study tips:

- **Do not do the assignment only once; repeat it several times.** If you are doing accounting problems or exercises, for example, do them a few times. Repetition of something is good for a kinesthetic/tactile learner.

- **Read ahead, using your finger to follow along for better concentration.**

- **Write questions to ask during lecture.**

- **Work on one subject at a time until it is finished.**

- **Make a list of topics to study.**

- **Break the material you need to learn into smaller increments, studying in chunks instead of all at once.**

- **Try to take frequent breaks when studying. You can easily be distracted and have trouble sitting still.**

- **Plan on studying for several sessions before a test.**

- **You are more apt to do your best studying in the morning.**

Can you have more than one learning style? Yes. The numbers on your score may show that you are very close in two areas or that you are fairly even in all three styles. Those are good results because they show that you are flexible and can learn in more than one way. You adjust easily to different teaching styles professors may have.

The learning style assessment you took was a very straightforward, simple one. More complex assessments are available. If you find the topic of learning styles interesting and want to learn more about it, check out the information in the appendix at the end of this book. It lists several books and Web sites where you can go to learn more about your learning style. You can also return to the site where you took your assessment:

http://www.metamath.com/lsweb/dvclearn.htm

Click on Learning Styles and Strategies to learn more about the results of your learning styles assessment.

When you discover your learning style and use the appropriate study tips, you will be on your way to becoming a more successful student.

Sources for Additional Help

If you continue to have problems understanding the material in a difficult class, you may want to see an academic coach or tutor. If your university or school does not offer an academic coach or tutor service, you may find some of the following suggestions useful.

- **Ask classmates or friends to clarify something you don't understand.** They may be able to explain it to you in a way that will help you understand the material.

- **Get together with other students in your class and start a study group or schedule a study session once a week.**

- **Look for additional materials on the subject at your campus or public library.** Libraries sometimes have videos and audiotapes in the subjects you are studying that can help you.

Personality Assessment

Personalities are like opinions; everyone has one. The word personality means this:

> "The totality of an individual's behavioral and emotional characteristics."

Finding out your personality type gives you a clearer picture of who you are. Earlier, we discussed perception and its effect on your success. We talked about how you may have sabotaged your academic success by listening to someone tell you that you aren't good at math. You may also have been conditioned about other things. You may have been told that you are shy or extremely clumsy. However, one of the greatest misconceptions people can have is their misconception about their personality.

You have been told so often and now believe that you are shy when in reality you could just be a quiet person. Or you may believe that you are stubborn. Some people are proud that they are stubborn. They say that it is in their genes to be stubborn. In reality, stubbornness is a personality trait and could be sabotaging you in many ways—one of which is to keep you from having an open mind toward learning new things. A personality assessment can reveal another piece of the puzzle as to who you are and the perception that you have of yourself.

Several personality assessments are available. The Jung Typology Test based on the Keirsey Personality Assessment, for example, has more than 70 questions. Consequently, it takes some time to complete it.

When you finish taking and scoring your assessment, you will get a four-letter personality type. You can go to the Web sites shown on your results page to read about the four-letter personality type you have.

The assessment will also give you some ideas about certain traits you may want to improve on. If you find that you are assessed as being extremely extroverted, for example, you may want to work on being more outgoing. Doing so could improve your career as well as your performance as a student. Please complete the following assignment before you finish reading this chapter.

Success Secret #3 Assignment 2: Take the Jung Typology Test

In this assignment, you complete a personality assessment that takes some effort. The reward is that the results can give you a basic awareness of your personality type.

1. Go to this Web site:

   http://www.humanmetrics.com/cgi-win/JTypes2.asp

   This Web link will take you directly to the Jung Typology Test.

2. Read through the statements slowly and mark the statement that best describes how you are most of the time.

(continued)

(continued)

3. After completing the assessment, click on Score It for a score.

4. Follow these directions carefully: After getting your score, you will see "Your Type Is" and then a four-letter sequence. You may see results that show you are an INFP or an IESJ or another four-letter type. You want to look for that four-letter sequence. This is your four-letter personality type.

5. Print this page. You will also be printing two other pages.

6. Look for two lines under your four-letter personality type. Those are links to other pages.

7. Click on the first link and print the page that appears, the portrait (description) of your personality type.

8. After you print that page, click the Back button and click on the next link, a profile of your personality type.

9. Print the profile. The three printed pages explain your personality type.

10. Save your printouts to share with your class.

11. Click on other links on the Web site to access additional information if you would like to read more on personalities.

The 16 personality types are

ESFP	ESFJ	ENFJ	ENTJ
ESTP	ESTJ	ENFP	ENTP
ISFP	ISFJ	INFJ	INTJ
ISTP	ISTJ	INFP	INTP

The following table describes Keirsey's 16 personality types and the meaning of the letters used in the personality assessment.

(continued)

(continued)

Keirsey's Sixteen Personality Types

Position	Letter	Description
First	E for Extrovert (75% of the population)	Are outgoing Draw energy from social activities Like to socialize Have many friends Talk first, think later Approachable Are drained by reflective thinking
	I for Introvert (25% of the population)	Are reserved Intense Listen more than talk Reflect before acting Enjoy quiet Are perceived to be a great listener Have few close friends but know them well Social activities tend to drain your energy
Second	N for Intuition (25% of the population)	Have a vivid imagination Like the unknown Like originality Get the whole picture from few facts Aren't easily motivated unless you anticipate something new Think of several things at once Give general answers to most questions Fantasize

Position	Letter	Description
	S for Sensing (75% of the population)	Look to the future Speculative Anything is possible Head-in-clouds Fantasize Imaginative
Third	T for Thinking (50% of the population)	Objective Principle oriented Policy oriented Laws Criterion-oriented Firmness Impersonal Justice oriented Categories Standards Critique Analysis Allocation
	F for Feeling (50% of the population)	Subjective Values Social values Extenuating circumstances Intimacy Persuasion Personal Humane Harmony Good or bad Appreciate Sympathy Devotion
Fourth	J for Judgment	Settled Decided Plan ahead

(continued)

(continued)

Keirsey's Sixteen Personality Types

Position	Letter	Description
	J for Judgment (cont.)	Run one's life
		Closure
		Decision making
		Planned
		Completed
		Decisive
		Wrap it up
		Urgency
		Deadline
		Get show on the road
	P for Perception	Pending
		Gather more data
		Flexible
		Adapt as you go
		Let life happen
		Open options
		Treasure hunting
		Open ended
		Emergent
		Tentative
		Something will turn up
		There's plenty of time
		What deadline?
		Let's wait and see

Once again, it is important that you understand that the test results may not be exact; but if you marked the statement stating how you are most of the time, they will be close. Also, remember everything is on a scale. You can be anywhere from 0 to 100 percent on that scale. If you are an I (Introvert), for example, you can be anywhere from extremely introverted to just a little introverted. If you have always thought you are an extrovert but your results are "I" for introvert, you are probably on the higher end of the Introvert scale and close to the Extrovert side.

Why take an assessment? Can personalities change? Sure they can. Age is one factor. You will find that the older people get, the less introverted they may become. Education is another factor in changing personalities. Someone who was extremely shy and introverted at one time may have taken some classes on how to be more outgoing. The assessments they take after learning how to be more outgoing will show different results.

Knowing your personality type will help you understand yourself better and in a more positive way, actually increasing your self-esteem. If you want to become more outgoing, for example, you can read self-help books on that subject. If you want to improve your logic or analytical skills, you can study methods of thinking. Most assessments list famous people who have the same personality type as you do.

Not only does that trivial information help you, but also knowing your personality type can even help you in the corporate world. Many companies give their employees personality assessments and occupational personality assessments to see which jobs they are best suited for and what areas they should be working in. For additional information on personalities, go to the following Web sites:

http://typelogic.com/

http://www.humanmetrics.com/

Other Assessments

Several other assessments are available to help you know yourself better. In high school, for example, you probably took an occupational personality assessment. That type of assessment is scored, and the results list professions suited to your personality type, based on the traits, characteristics, and skills you believe you have. Other occupational assessments frequently given are the *Transition-to-Work Inventory* by Dr. John Liptak and SIGI PLUS, which creates a list of occupations based on your values, interests, and work skills. Another assessment in this area is the Occupational Personality Questionnaire (OPQ) that is designed to provide information on the typical behavior of an individual within work situations. Some of the questions these assessments answer are

- Can you work well with others?

- Do you enjoy being around people?

- Can you solve problems and assess difficult situations?

Administrators find that using these assessments helps them decide which people they should choose for specific jobs. If an assessment such as *Self-Directed Search* by John Holland shows that you are extremely introverted, you may be best suited for a job with little contact with other people. Other Web sites that discuss assessments in this area are

http://www.jist.com

http://careerplanning.about.com/cs/selfassessment

Another assessment that is quick to take (no more than five minutes), fun, and revealing is the Lüscher Color Test. Dr. Max Lüscher studied color psychology, how color affects behavior. He found that certain colors cause an emotional response in people. The test itself is based on his findings. Such a test can reveal both short-term and long-term personality characteristics and is affected by your emotional state at the time of the test. If you are feeling down or depressed and take the test, those emotions might be reflected in your results. They vary each time you take the test, so the validity is not specific, but it is accurate. While this test is used in European countries and overseas, the U.S. has few experts on this test, though some corporations use the Lüscher Color Test as part of the hiring process. You can find the Lüscher Color Test at this Web site:

http://www.colorquiz.com/

We were really amazed when we took this color test and received the results. They gave what was referred to as "your existing situation," which was very accurate. We learned what our stress sources are, our restrained characteristics, our desired objective, and our actual problem areas. It was fun and gave us a little bit of insight into our current situations.

Perception, Learning Styles, and Personality Conclusion

After reading this chapter and completing the assessments, you should know yourself much better. Now that you know your learning style, you can choose the correct way to study. If you have more than one learning style, you can even be more successful with your studies because you have even more tools to use.

This chapter gave you methods of gaining insight into who you really are. Understanding yourself can reduce preconceived self-perceptions that may not be true. It is fun to find out "how" you really are.

Best Practices Summary
Do's and Don'ts of Success Secret #3
Perception, Learning Styles, and Personality

Do

- Do understand how your perceptions can keep you from being successful.
- Do take learning style and personality assessments.
- Do be honest in marking your assessments.
- Do mark your assessments in terms of how you are most of the time.
- Do read the results of your assessments with an open mind.
- Do peruse some additional readings on personality and learning styles.
- Do get to know yourself better.

Don't

- Don't let others tell you how or who you are. Be your own person.
- Don't let others tell you where you want to be and what you want to do.
- Don't mark your answers on the assessment in terms of how you "want to be."

CHAPTER 4

Success Secret #4: Organization

"We have become a society of dilly-dallyers."

from *Guilt Free Goofing Off* by Brian Bergman

Here is an interesting saying: "If you want something done, ask the busiest person you know to do it." In other words, productive people are often the most organized.

Like most students, you probably have too much on your plate. This most likely will become more evident after you learn the time management strategies and do the assignments in this chapter. If you feel that you are lacking in these skills, fear not—you too can learn them. With a little practice, a new tool can become a habit in about 21 days.

Start with Your Location

Choose a good location to study. Make it one that

- Is conducive to focusing because it is free of noise and clutter.
- Suits your learning style.
- Isn't too comfortable (in other words, not on the couch or curled up on a bed).

When you choose a location for studying that lets you be productive, you give your work the respect and importance it deserves. However, no matter how carefully you choose your location, you're likely to run into problems. Here are our problem-solving tips:

- **Take notes while you study so that you tune out distractions and stay focused.**

- **Minimize distractions by turning off the TV or getting earplugs.**

- **Let voice mail or the answering machine handle phone calls.** You would not answer your cell phone in any class (we hope), so why not let the answering machine take (or at least screen) your calls while you are studying?

- **If you have too many distractions in your room or at home, go to the library.** It's usually a fairly quiet study environment.

Monitor Your Schedule

Organize and monitor study sessions to get the most out of each one. To do that, apply these suggestions:

- **Start your assignments early so you can have extra (flex) time in case something unexpected comes along or if you get stuck at some difficult point.** This flex time will be your saving grace at some point in your college experience.

- **To gain even more flex time, schedule more work for the first half of each course week rather than the latter half.**

- **Make yourself familiar with the routine of the lessons.** Successful students advise you to read each assignment first and glance through the rest of the material, so you know what is coming down the pike.

- **Depending on your energy level, you will likely find it more enjoyable if you do the easy parts quickly.** That way you will accomplish more in a shorter period of time.

- **Pay attention to the details.** Know in advance when the assignments are going to be due and how much they are weighted toward your total points.

- **Make certain that all your assignments, tests, and quizzes are completed by the designated due date.** The instructor does not get paid less or more whether you pass or fail the course.

- **Set a pattern: Think through how you're going to complete each assignment.**

- **Create a plan for completing each assignment.** Because most instructors take points off for late work, find out what your instructor's policy is, know the due date for the assignment, and plan backward from there so that you know the steps you need to take and the dates you need to complete them. That way you'll stay on target.

- **Check your work.**

- **After you turn in your work, check your grades and answers to make sure you are on the right track.**

Successful students also advise that you review what you did the previous week before continuing to the next week, to refresh your memory of what you have covered and to tie it to what you will be learning. Also, remember that you must review or see new material eight times before your brain crystallizes it.

Organize Logistically

Logistics is simply mapping out a plan of class organization that is time efficient. It is the same principle you can apply when taking a vacation trip. If you are traveling from New York City to Los Angeles, for example, it is best to travel the straightest line possible. You usually would not want to go to Kentucky and backtrack to Maine, then head to Ohio, down to Texas, and back to Missouri. Getting to LA would take you forever!

The logistical organization of your studying should be no different. Simply make a list that is most practical to navigate the course content. Some students advocate logistically organizing those course items that are the highest priority in the class first. These are most often quizzes, tests, and assignments. For example, put all assignments, quizzes, and tests on a calendar so you know what is coming up and can prepare for them in advance.

Whatever logistical method you choose to get through your class, it is important that you don't miss any stops along the way. Furthermore, another best practice is to determine whether you have the most efficient and effective logistical map after you have spent some time in the class. Predict the amount of time you need to do your assignments and then see if you can beat that time! We are not giving you permission to rush to the point that you do shabby work; we're suggesting that you try to work effectively and efficiently without being sloppy. Predicting and monitoring your time spent on assignments will give you an indication of how organized you are.

If you develop a plan and stick to it, the time you spend studying for class should be reduced, assuming that you have a similar workload from week to week. When you reduce your studying time, your logistical organization plan is working. However, if your number of assignments increases, you will need to revamp your organizational plan.

Success Secret #4 Assignment 1: Create a Logistical Organization

For this assignment, you make a simple plan of what you need to do for class.

1. List all the assignments you have and when exams are coming up.

2. Rate your assignments by priority from most to least important.

3. Work on those of high priority.

4. Choose a method of going through your prioritized list—from top to bottom, or left to right, or a combination that works for you.

5. Organize your plan into a daily or weekly schedule.

6. When you complete your list, try it out.

7. Keep a record of how long it takes you to finish assignments for classes you have organized and those you don't have organized. Assuming similar workloads, your time should decrease as you become more proficient in managing your time and adept at following your organizational map.

8. Be prepared to share this list with the class.

Additional Secrets from Successful Students

We polled some successful students for strategies they use to keep themselves organized. Their tips include the following:

- **Do your assignments early in the week.** If something comes up later in the week, you will already have your course work completed, and you'll have one less thing to worry about.

- **Plan ahead so that you can complete your large projects early and review them before you actually submit them.**

- **Spend a little time each day reading your assignments.** This will help you concentrate on what you are reading so you are focusing on the material you need for your assignments. Otherwise, you will most likely miss half or more of what you read.

- **Spend a little time each day reading over your assignment requirements.** Otherwise, you will most likely miss important parts of the assignments.

- **Time yourself when you read.** See how long it takes you to read 5 to 10 pages so that you can accurately estimate how long you need for your study sessions.

- **Do extra research on the tough assignments, using the library or resources that are available online.**

- **Don't overwork.**

- **Set a stopping time, forcing yourself to work in a more focused manner.**

Special Organizational Situations

We do not all enter college at the same time of life. Nor are we all on-campus students. This section shares organizational tips for two special situations: Students who have families and online students.

Organize Around Families

If you have a family, you may need to organize your studying around caring for them. Here are some suggestions:

- **Make a balanced, win-win plan with your family for your study time so that they have a reason to give you the space and time you need.** In other words, negotiate a "reward" for giving you study time.

- **Set a timer and then do what you said you would do.**

- **If you are studying and have small children, take frequent breaks and make certain the children have good things to occupy their time.**

- **Arrange a co-op with another parent.** You can take turns swapping study time for childcare.

- **Know your limits and be somewhat realistic about your course load.** Take a little longer to finish your degree so that you are able to have a nicer journey along the way.

Here is what works for one successful student: He organizes toys, snacks, and a movie for his children to keep them content while he studies. They all plan an activity they will do together when he takes a break. He is always thinking "win-win."

Organize for Online Learning

So what are the secret pearls of wisdom other successful online students advise to get organized? Here is what they say:

- Most online classes have some type of orientation. When the class first starts, make sure you complete the orientation. If it's optional, do it anyway.

- Most online classes have some type of "Start Here" section when you actually start the class. Pay attention to it. This section can make or break you because it shows you how to easily navigate online.

- Every day when you first log on, go through your new e-mail, check grades, and check the discussion board before you begin the next segment.

- Stay with the assigned schedule or work ahead if it is allowed.

- Make sure you take part in any scheduled chat room discussion and post to the class online discussion board. These areas make the course more fun and usually are graded.

- Print the more challenging assignments and have them handy so you can think about them for a couple of days. Soon they will be familiar and not look so hard anymore.

- Break the more difficult assignments into smaller pieces.

- Don't assume that you know it all and skim through the material. Let the work sink into you.

- Do all your assignments and take enough time to make them meaningful.

- Logistically organize online work, based on proximity. If the grade book is left of the online discussion tab, for example, some students check the grade book first and then go to the online discussion tab.

- Develop an organizational pattern in the class and follow it step by step. If you do the steps in the order set forth, the assignments will most likely build on each other and it is less likely that you will forget one.

- If your online class gives you a checklist for each chapter or unit, print the list and cross off the items when you have them completed. See the sample daily/weekly checklist that follows.

Each day check

- ❑   Class e-mail
- ❑   Announcement center
- ❑   Weekly assignments
- ❑   For quizzes or tests
- ❑   Threaded discussion
- ❑   Turned-in assignments in the drop box
- ❑   Gradebook
- ❑   Document-sharing area and/or online library
- ❑   Course objectives
- ❑   Big project status (in other words, term projects or papers)
- ❑   Weekly online lecture material
- ❑   Online chat room scheduled discussions

Organization Conclusion

Just as you plan your vacation or your future, you need to plan and organize your classes in order to succeed. If you try to succeed without an organized plan, we guarantee you will miss something. Planning will get you the results you want—within a shorter time span. Do you remember Murphy's Laws? Yes, more than one Murphy's Law exists. Here are just a few.

Nothing is as easy as it looks.

Everything takes longer than you think it will.

Anything that can go wrong will go wrong.

If anything simply can't go wrong, it will anyway.

Left to themselves, things tend to go from bad to worse.

If you want to read more, go to this Web site:

http://dmawww.epfl.ch/roso.mosaic/dm/murphy.html

Being well-prepared requires that we each take the responsibility for our own success. Even though we would like to and sometimes do lean on others, we are responsible. If you practice these organizational tools frequently, they will become habits, and your potential will be unleashed.

Best Practices Summary
Do's and Don'ts of Success Secret #4
Organization

Do

- Do organize your workspace. Knowing where your equipment is optimizes your time.

- Do limit your distractions. Plan ahead to determine when and where you will find the quietest location.

- Do balance your life. Take time for family, friends, hobbies, and so on. Doing so will make you more efficient and effective.

(continued)

(continued)

- Do develop a logistical plan. (For online students, decide whether you will go to the thread discussion area first; then check e-mail, grades, assignments, and so on.) You should stick to the plan unless your time efficiency drops.

- Do organize your assignments. Begin them early in the week so you have flex time that may be needed later in the week.

- Do choose to do easy or hard assignments first depending on your energy level. If your energy is high, successful students usually choose to do the hard assignments first.

- Do use a checklist. Whether you print the syllabus or a formal class checklist, keep it handy and mark off the tasks as you complete them each week.

Don't

- Don't minimize the importance of an organized plan. If you do, you will waste time and perform below your potential.

- Don't over-organize your life. Some people spend too much time developing a time management strategy and never do anything. Over-organizing is counterproductive. Just get an organizational plan together, stick to it, and tweak it only if needed. Don't become obsessive with organizing.

- Don't let yourself become overwhelmed. If you do, you will freeze up and be unable to accomplish anything effectively or efficiently.

Success Secret #4 Assignment 2: Organize Your Week

For this assignment, you organize your assignments for one week.

1. Use a checklist of assignments that are due for that week to organize yourself.

2. Write down each assignment and what you need to do to finish it.

3. Check the assignment off as you finish it, making a note to your-self of whether studying went better because you were organized and knew that you were staying on top of things.

4. Save your checklist to share with the class.

CHAPTER 5

Success Secret #5: Attitude

"You are never given a wish without also being given the power to make it come true. You may have to work for it, however."

Richard Bach

So you want to get a degree? Have you actually asked yourself why? If the answer is anything other than "I want to," then you are not ready to dive in headfirst. If you would rather be doing other things, you will be distracted from your studies and will likely fail.

Conversely, when you are mentally committed to being a student, the rest falls into place. It's all about attitude. Attitude breeds commitment. Commitment leads to motivation. Motivation leads to success. It is all interrelated and very important for your success.

Realize That Input Equals Output

You get out of your classes exactly what you put into them. If your attitude toward education is positive, you will receive a positive experience and education. However, if your attitude is negative, you will have a negative experience and education. As with most things in life, you get to decide. It's all up to you and your attitude.

Mother Teresa has been quoted as saying, "Do it anyway." Nike uses the famous words "Just Do It" in its advertising. Essentially, those principles are appropriately linked to education. Here's what we mean:

- Getting a degree is a difficult task. . . "Do it anyway."

- Getting a degree requires time management and organizational skills. . . "Do it anyway."

- Some classes require specific computer skills. . . "Do it anyway."

- I have to take this required class, but I really don't need or want to. . . "Do it anyway."

- I don't want to study. I'd rather go to a party with friends or to a movie. . . "Do it anyway."

The premise here, of course, is that you must adopt an attitude of empowerment and ability. Despite the fact that you might have other things you would rather do than go to class and participate, do it anyway and tell yourself you want to.

You lean in the direction you feel strongly about. If you want that degree, keep affirming to yourself, "I can do this." If you say that to yourself often enough and really want it, you will do it.

If you have a positive attitude, you will lean toward the positive outcome. If you have a negative attitude, you will make up all kinds of reasons not to accomplish your goal. There are only two reasons people do not accomplish their goals:

- They *don't* want it badly enough.

- They *can't* see themselves doing it.

See those negative words: don't and can't? Get rid of them. If you want it badly enough and can see yourself doing it (or have the vision), you can do anything. Having a positive attitude will get you the kind of success you want.

Use Patience to Produce Results

In class, sometimes you don't "get it" right away. Cultivate the habit of patience. Patience is a sign of your personal maturity. You cope better with your everyday studies if you balance your life and maintain a patient perspective.

Don't force things to happen. Wait. This does not mean that you should procrastinate. Not at all. What you are after is a feeling of serenity and calm. When you are calm, you can retain more of what you learn, and you will be a person whom others enjoy being around. Procrastination, on the other hand, is just a result of negative thinking. If you tell yourself you *have* to do something, it is the same as if someone else has said that to you. Your subconscious pushes back, and you start thinking of all types of creative ways to get out of doing it.

Instead of becoming frustrated and impatient with their classroom experience, successful students advise others to adopt an attitude and mentality of challenge. Instead of complaining that your instructor doesn't promptly answer your questions, thank him or her for giving you and other class members the opportunity to find the answers on your own. The need for answers gives students the opportunity to reach out and make friends, as well as learn to work as a team.

If this reasoning seems far-fetched to you, then think of students who are successful. They reach out to others and get the help they need. They either start a study group or see if they can locate a tutor or an academic coach.

One thing you will find in your classes is a group of people in the same situations you are in. They have daily commitments in addition to being in school that affect their attitudes. Get together and discuss these difficulties. Become one another's support team. These discussions provide a perfect time to ask questions about how they get their assignments done and still maintain sanity. If you make a connection with a class member, perhaps the class itself will become more exciting.

Make Good Impressions

Keep in mind that you are making an impression on your instructors with every assignment you turn in. Instructors don't take long to find out who has a good attitude about the class. That attitude *will* make a difference in the student's success. Chronic complainers quickly become the students who are having a difficult time. To be honest, these students don't often get the breaks others do. In fact, we have noticed that other students in the class don't communicate often with the complainers. A poor attitude conveyed through actions hurts only the one with the attitude. Successful students advise others to check their attitudes at the door before they come to class.

Here's an important reason for making a good impression: You may want your professors and/or fellow classmates for references for scholarships and future jobs. Furthermore, those students who decide to go on to graduate school *have* to ask instructors to recommend them. Make sure you have the attitude you need to get the reference or recommendation you want. Instructors usually have many connections and can help you network as you seek your future position. Your positive attitude will go a long way toward ensuring an instructor's or classmate's willingness to stand up for you.

Be Tough

Sometimes you will hear a comment from your instructor or classmates that might offend you. Take the time and have the courage to discuss the perceived offense further; you probably will find that those who made the comments had good intentions.

Part of classroom etiquette is not to be hasty in judgment. And it's great advice. Always give people the benefit of the doubt. Assume that all communications are honorable in their intent until absolutely proven otherwise. In other words, don't automatically take every word personally. Some successful students have even commented that it's more than just attitude: "You must have the hide of a rhino," they say.

Be aggressive when it comes to class. Get mentally tough. Your mental toughness will ensure that you get what you want. Keep at it. Remember to revisit that vision of why you are in school—to get that degree. Don't lose that vision. Take all setbacks as temporary, including a bad grade, computer problems, or personal conflicts. When setbacks happen, get in touch with your instructor or school immediately. Let someone know what is going on. That person will often have ideas to assist you through the setback. Do not let setbacks become an excuse to quit. Enough said.

Focus on Your Strengths

Become committed to YOU! You deserve the best of everything that you seek. Never sell yourself short. Who signed up for the class in the first place? The toughest part of getting the degree for some is just signing up for the class. You are the reason you are working so hard. Your strengths will see you through. And, one of the most important strengths all of us have is the ability to be motivated and motivate ourselves.

See your motivation as strength by asking yourself WIIFM (what's in it for me). When you know your WIIFM, you can use it as a driving force. You commit to other things in your life the same way. Think about it. You are taking classes because you believe that doing so will help you get where you want to go. Attitudes of success and motivation are developed, not genetic. You can develop a "can-do" attitude.

You can learn any subject. The people who become successful and have astonishing results at meeting their goals are average people who learned and applied the tools to success. If you find that you say, "I can't do it," change it by adding a "yet." I can't do it "YET." It's "yet" another primary success principle.

Have you heard the saying, "Can't didn't, but try always won"? Those who try are winners because they tried. Those who don't try don't give themselves the opportunity to win. They have already lost.

Challenge the Challenges

Do not let temporary and minor setbacks distract you from your work and goals. You can find creative solutions to these problems. You are actually at your creative best when you have a problem.

Another success principle is applicable here. "Failure is success turned inside out." This is to say that your problems, setbacks, and "failures" are really just successes turned inside out. Why? Because successful students learn from their failures, they think outside the box for creative solutions to their problems, setbacks, and failures.

Do not be disheartened by getting things wrong. When you make a mistake on a quiz or assignment, move on. You remember those sayings "don't give up the ship" and "one day at a time"? So what if you have a setback? Pull yourself up, dust yourself off, and smile. Don't think of it as a failure, but as part of the learning process. You are allowed imperfections. They are part of life and can lead to a new growth level for you. Just start over tomorrow.

Be Aware of Scotomas

Be aware of *scotomas* (blind spots). Scotomas are blind spots that directly affect your attitude. A typical scotoma that successful students have identified and overcome is one that limits abilities. For example, many students cannot initially see the value of a learner-centered environment until they actually experience it. Others have a difficult time seeing why it's so important to manage their time and organize their life until they cannot complete an assignment or project on time. The secret key to identifying and removing scotomas is to think outside the box that creates blind spots in your life.

The trouble with being inside a limiting box is that the directions on how to make your life better are outside of the box. This limitation is why you will want to examine your life and study successful people. The tools in this book are one way to get out of your box in terms of what you can do with your academic program. Another way to get out of your scotoma box is to change your daily routine. For example, pick a different way to drive home from work or the game. Open your mind to new possibilities. Highly effective students have an open mind, and they "see" or are willing to see endless possibilities and the truth about themselves. This openness makes them successful.

Dare to Be Great

The difference between mediocrity and greatness is infinitesimally small. The difference between first place and last place in a NASCAR race is often less than four seconds. *Four* seconds! The difference between first and second place is often less than a tenth of a second!

The difference between a great baseball hitter and an average hitter is equally small. Those who bat .500 or above are considered great—a very small percentage of major league baseball players. Mediocre professional baseball players normally bat between .200 and .350. The difference between great and mediocre here is often less than one extra hit every three or four games.

The difference between the winner and loser in the Masters PGA golf championship is normally less than 10 strokes over three days of golf. The difference between first and second place in the Masters is nearly always one stroke over three days of golf.

The question here is what makes the difference between mediocrity and greatness. The answer is simple—just a little extra effort. A little extra effort in improving your studying and test-taking skills. A little extra effort in your organizational skills. A little extra effort in developing a great attitude.

Attitude Conclusion

Attitude is about believing in yourself, knowing that if others (thousands and thousands of others) can get through school, so can you! Be willing to learn from your mistakes. Do not quit. Tell yourself you will do it differently and better next time.

Change your self-talk. Tell yourself that you are going to pass with a good grade. Tell yourself that you do have time. Tell yourself that you can and will do it. Remember what Henry Ford said: "Whether you think you can or you think you can't, you are right." So think you can. Tell yourself that your assignments are challenging, not hard. No matter how much you desire a positive outcome, you will sabotage your efforts if you don't *believe* you can do it. Think positively about the outcome, and you may need to fake this attitude until it becomes a habit.

Best Practices Summary
Do's and Don'ts of Success Secret #5
Attitude

Do

- Do develop an attitude of success. Successful students think, plan, and talk success.

- Do be patient, but persistent.

- Do challenge yourself and the challenges that face you. Develop an "I can" attitude and implement it always.

- Do focus on ability and possibility. Be self-confident and visualize your dreams.

- Do use the words, "try," "yet," and "want to." Empower your subconscious to give you abilities you never knew you had.

- Do recognize your scotomas (blind spots). Open your eyes to new possibilities based on positive attitude adjustments.

- Do be tough. Give others the benefit of the doubt until proven otherwise.

(continued)

(continued)

Don't

- Don't succumb to self-doubt. If you don't think you can, you probably can't.

- Don't give up. Learn to roll with the punches and get up, dust yourself off, and move ahead.

- Don't settle for mediocrity. Don't sell yourself short of excellence. Go the extra few inches to become great.

Success Secret #5 Assignment 1: Identify Your Blind Spots

In this assignment, you identify five things you don't think you can do, and then identify the blind spots that prevent you from seeing the solutions. By doing this, you offer yourself a "can-do" attitude and literally ensure your success as a student.

1. Write down the five things you don't think you can do.

2. Identify the blind spots preventing you from accomplishing your five goals.

3. Save this list to share with your class.

CHAPTER 6

Success Secret #6: Goal Setting

"Good plans (goals) shape good decisions. That's why good planning helps to make elusive dreams come true."

Lester R. Bittel,
The Nine Master Keys of Management

Highly effective students must be goal oriented. You need to be able to see the light at the end of the tunnel, and, no, it is not a train coming at you. Remaining goal oriented can be difficult if you are a student who is plugging away at your degree, all the while juggling many responsibilities. If you are a non-traditional student, you probably have a job you are contending with, classes, and family. You are expected to be in 20 places at once.

The same applies to traditional students. You might have classes, as well as a family of your own, or family stresses far away. You might be in collegiate sports programs or in a very study-intensive program. You might even have to take a part-time or full-time job to meet your financial needs. You also need to find a way to see the end, to keep in mind the success principle that states, "You will move toward what you think about."

If you try to maintain a positive attitude but don't have a goal in mind, your student experience will remain an elusive dream.

Set SMART Goals

Successful students always set goals. One suggestion for setting goals is to write your goals on your calendar or put them in your electronic calendar. Before you do, make sure your goals are "SMART." SMART stands for:

Specific

Measurable

Attainable

Realistic

Tangible

Is your goal specific? A goal that is vague, such as "Get better grades," does not fill the bill for a good goal. A specific goal, such "Get an A in Accounting 102," does fill the bill for a good goal.

Is your goal measurable? Something that is not measurable is generally not attainable. The preceding example of the goal to "Get an A in Accounting 102" is measurable in that it states an "A" letter grade.

Is your goal attainable? Is it really something you can have, or just a pipe dream? For example, an unattainable goal for most of us would be "Become the King of England after completing my degree." Something more attainable might be "Become a vice president of XYZ Technology company after completing my MBA degree."

Is your goal realistic? While it is closely related to the standard of setting an attainable goal, this check forces us to look a little deeper. In the preceding example, if one of the requirements of becoming a vice president for XYZ Technology is four years of on-the-job experience and you have only six months of experience, the goal is probably not realistic unless you qualify it to include ". . . gain three more years of experience and . . ." It is good to have high expectations of yourself, but just keep them real. It can go the other way also. If you get a four-year degree, raise your expectations. Know you are going to get a better job than working for minimum wage at the local drive-through fast food restaurant.

Is your goal tangible? Is it something you can touch, feel, see, taste, or smell? A degree is tangible. When you have that diploma in your hand and the job offer of your dreams, you will understand just how tangible it is.

See the End

Making goals is easier if you look at the end first. What do you want to do when you graduate? What kind of degree do you want? What kind of lifestyle do you want? The dreams that you are visualizing will help you set goals. Keep your "eye on the prize." Remind yourself often of the larger picture, and focus on that positive outcome, whether it be a better job, new home, more money, or being a positive role model for your children. Just remember what your goals are.

As you establish long-range goals, you should also set short-range ones. Decide what you want to get out of each course you take and how it can improve you. Think of how what you are learning will apply to your career. It may help for you to post a list of your goals in the area where you are studying. Include the grade you are working toward, or the degree you are seeking. Seeing the "prize" in writing near your place of study or in a place you frequently look (such as on the mirror) will help you concentrate on both the long-term and short-term goals.

Check Your Attitude

After you set your goals, make sure your attitude takes you closer to your goals. If you need a session to complain, give yourself one, but time it (less than 15 minutes) and warn people around you that you are taking one. Then go for it. Let your frustration out. Remember to use this as a storm clears the air; use your complaining session to clear your mind and then get back to the task at hand. Laugh at yourself after your complaining session. One thing you will learn is that if you work toward your goal, you can have a serious attitude, a happy attitude, or whatever attitude you choose, but if you keep working toward your goals, you will get there.

"If you plant watermelon seeds and work the field, it does not matter whether you are in a certain mood; you will get watermelons."

That being said, you may have a more enjoyable process if you and others like your moods. That is a choice. But to stay positive means to believe in yourself and work toward your goals. The point is to keep working. Do something—anything—to take you to your goal. It has been said that persistence is the blood brother to success. Rest if needed, but keep at it.

Keep your goals and desires in the back and front of your mind. When you focus on a problem or beat yourself up with your own negative self-talk, immediately replace it with a constructive thought. Remember that problems are often opportunities in disguise. Stumbling blocks are just stepping stones in disguise.

Have Faith

We have all heard the cliché, "You gotta have faith." And successful students have identified faith as an important ingredient for setting goals. Faith is by definition ". . . the substance of things hoped for and the evidence of things not seen" (Hebrews 11:1). In other words, faith is confidence and trust that you can and will be more than you currently are. Trust and confidence are the keys to faith. . .the keys to knowing and believing you will succeed even though you are not there yet.

An analogy for understanding faith follows the story of a young driver who has completed driver's education, the driver's examination, and three months of experience on the open road and in the city streets. This young person is confident in his abilities. He trusts his judgment, and others trust his skills. However, when the snow flies for the first time and the streets become icy, the question is asked, "Do I have faith (confident trust) that I can make it from point A to point B in these conditions?"

Have faith in knowing that, when the streets become slippery and you choose to drive in the lane of education, the question is asked, "Do I have faith (confident trust) that I can obtain my degree, job, and lifestyle goals in any conditions?" The answer is a resounding "Yes!" So what if you put it in the ditch a time or two? As long as you are willing to learn from your mistakes and press on, you will succeed.

Recognize That a Goal Without Work Is a Wish

When you sit down to think of your goals, make them realistic enough to see them, yet far enough out to give you the creative drive to get them. If you are setting goals too close to what you actually know you can attain, then your life will remain the same. Tomorrow will look a lot like yesterday. You want to do both: Have clear and realistic, attainable goals, as well as making large goals and then chunking them into smaller goals, like stepping stones.

You can follow the success principle that states, "You will move toward and become like that which you think about the most and with the strongest emotions." When you know what you want, visualize it, and know it is yours. Picture yourself having or accomplishing that goal. What you focus on will expand, so focus on goals and the life you seek. Remember, the life you seek is also seeking you.

To get the drive to go where you want to go, set some "in a perfect life" goals. What would you have, do, or be if you were living your perfect life? Suspend your critical mind and write down some goals that you have a passion for. Forget about the "how." Just write them down. You can expand this beyond your academic goals, as they will support each other. In other words, if you have a goal of having a certain income, then getting your degree might be a step in that direction. Just make short-term goals for your classes.

Success Secret #6 Assignment 1: Identify the Negatives

Before you can proceed in the direction of your dreams, you must identify the negatives that hold you back. In this assignment, you not only identify the negatives; you turn them inside out until they are positives.

1. Get a piece of paper, and write down all the things that are negatives in your life right now. What are the things that wear you down, scare you, and or make you sad?

(continued)

(continued)

2. Get another sheet of paper and, like reversing a negative of a picture, take each item and reverse it. What is the opposite? If you wrote down that you don't have enough money to pay your bills, write down that you have more than enough money to pay your bills easily. Keep writing until you have reversed all your negative.

3. Go back and make all the positives specific. Envision a true story for your life.

4. Date this piece of paper and put it someplace where you can look at it often.

Success Secret #6 Assignment 2: Recognize the Consequences

Based on the assumption that you have a goal of graduating, this assignment helps you focus on why graduating is more important than quitting. The result should enable you to work more effectively and efficiently toward your goal.

1. Get two pieces of paper, and then draw a horizontal line in the middle of each paper, dividing it in half.

2. On each piece of paper, draw a vertical line that divides the upper half into two sections. You should end up with two quarters in the top half and one full half in the lower half of each paper.

3. Write conflicting goals at the top of each paper. For example, you could put "Classes/Graduate" on one paper and "Work More" on the other.

(continued)

(continued)

4. For each goal, list its advantages or the reasons you could choose it in the left upper quarter of the paper. (If you get stuck, you might ask others to help you with your list.)

5. In the right quarter, write or list the inconveniences, disadvantages, or reasons that the goal is not a good option.

6. After you list the positives and negatives, write the "future" in the bottom section of each paper.

7. Using the lists of positives and negatives, write the results of following any of the lines of thinking.

When you see these results written in black and white, you can foresee the results of each. You are then able to set goals that are based on the choices you need to make to have the future you desire.

The purpose of these exercises is to get you beyond inertia. They can put motivation behind your goals. After you plot this out, it is no longer a dream. It is not based on your imagination. It is your future reality.

Always ask yourself if what you are about to do takes you away from your goals or closer to them. If it is further away, just say "no."

Plan Ahead for Setbacks

Having obstacles in your path is not a bad thing. In fact, it has been said that hitting roadblocks and feeling frustrated is a sign that you chose worthy goals: You want them! If you can predict those roadblocks, all the better; you can anticipate in advance how you might get through them. Think about what might go wrong and how you would deal with it. What will you do, for example, if your computer crashes? You can ask friends if you can use their computers. You can also find a computer lab in the library you can use. Now you are ready to let that potential road-block go to the side, because what you focus on expands, and worrying is actually negative goal setting.

If you are expecting everything to go smoothly all the time, you are going to be disappointed. Rather, see the problems as opportunities to reach your goals. Success is usually failure turned inside out, so do not be dismayed by setbacks.

Reward Yourself

When you achieve a goal, remember to give yourself a reward—no matter how small. Have fun and learn to celebrate your successes! Make sure that you tell yourself how proud you are that you received a good grade on your paper or test. Give yourself some treat, such as an ice cream cone for a small achievement or a larger treat for a greater achievement: Get a new outfit, go to a movie, or whatever you choose. Just make sure you do some thing so that your subconscious will continue to strive to achieve the rewards.

For Online Students

Most online students are taking classes on the Internet because they lack time to attend classes in a traditional setting. It is very important for online students to remember that they must succeed as self-directed learners. They may not have the same prodding that on-campus students have. Their professor and friends aren't in their faces, reminding them that they need to be in class, when assignments are due, and where they should be in their reading. Online students have to keep track of it all and make sure it gets done.

You know how to organize, you have your study skills tools and test-taking tools, you know your learning style and personality type, and you have a positive attitude. Now take it one step further and set goals. As an online student, you are responsible. Set goals as to when you are going to finish assignments and where you should be at specific dates on your calendar. You may find it difficult at the beginning of that first semester or quarter to remember that you are responsible for your success and when things need to be done. Review the goal-setting tools and you can have your cake and eat it too! Successful online students always set goals.

Goal Setting Conclusion

Visualize the long- and short-term picture of your success. With each class, remember the end goal and keep visualizing yourself attaining it. If your goal is getting a degree, graduating with honors, or attaining financial independence, see yourself already there. Consider taking a picture of yourself in a cap and gown. When you see the end result, you can keep going even (or rather, especially) when you face obstacles.

Best Practices Summary
Do's and Don'ts of Success Secret #6 Goal Setting

Do

- Do see the end. Find out where you want to go, and you will get there as you set goals.

- Do write SMART goals. Vague and unspecific goals will result in a vague and unspecific experience.

- Do think both long- and short-term. There are important victories to be had in meeting short-term goals that can propel you toward the long-term ones.

- Do check your attitude. It really doesn't matter what your attitude is for a short amount of time as long as others are fairly warned and you continue to plow the field.

- Do have faith in yourself. Be confident in your abilities and trust that you will succeed.

- Do recognize failure as an opportunity to succeed. As long as you are humble enough to learn from your mistakes, failure is always success turned inside out.

- Do reward yourself. Celebrate achievements. Celebrating is more important than most people think.

Don't

- Don't think you can't. If you think you can't, then you won't. It's as simple and as difficult as that.

- Don't begin without seeing the end. Short-term goals without long-term dreams, vision, and goals will short-change you.

- Don't expect goal achievement without work. Without work, goals are just a dream.

Success Secret #6 Assignment 3: Search the Web for Goal Setting

1. Using the search engine of your choice, locate a Web site that deals with goal setting. You can use the following links:

   http://www.mindtools.com/page6.html

   http://www.mygoals.com/index.html?1003

   http://www.mygoalmanager.com/

2. Find three helpful tips you would use in goal setting.

3. Write down the URL of the Web site and the three tips to share with your class.

CHAPTER 7

Success Secret #7: Basic Research Skills

"By seeking and blundering we learn."

Johann Wolfgang von Goethe

As you go through your academic career, you will be asked this question more and more frequently: "Are you information literate?" Are you familiar with the term information literate?

Information Literacy

The American Library Association defines information literacy as "the set of abilities requiring individuals to recognize when information is needed and have the ability to locate, evaluate, and use effectively the needed information." The association has listed nine information literacy standards for student learning. These standards help students to develop:

- Information literacy
- Independent learning
- Social responsibility

To read the nine standards, you can go to the following Web site:
www.ala.org/aasl/ip_nine.html

You will realize how important it is to become information literate in all aspects of your life. Many people, including educators, are not information literate. Get a step ahead and make sure that you are. Be able to find the information you need.

We live in a society in which people want information, but they want it now and they want someone else to get it for them. Don't fall into the trap of "fast is better." Don't expect anyone to hold your hand and guide you to the information you need. Take the responsibility for conducting your own research. This doesn't mean that you can't get help. You just can't learn how to find information if you aren't willing to do the work. When you get the hang of finding information and are comfortable with using a variety of sources of information, you will be surprised how much knowledge you will gain. You will increase your academic potential by leaps and bounds. For more information on information literacy, you can go to this Web site:

http://www.ala.org/ala/acrl/acrlstandards/
informationliteracycompetency.cfm

Becoming information literate means not only that you can find information, but also that you can use critical thinking skills. Critical thinking, put simply, is problem solving.

At the university level, you will have to write research papers and complete projects during your academic career. As the standards state, you need to be able to find information from a variety of sources, sort through and organize that information, form opinions about it, and write research papers at the university and college level without plagiarizing (using someone else's information, passing it off as your own, and not giving credit to the source where you found that information). When you learn how to do research, writing research papers becomes second nature.

Reading this chapter isn't going to make you a research genius, but it will guide you and give you information that will help you do a better job in deciding how to find reliable, valid information. You won't feel so "dazed and confused" by all the sources of information available to you. The chapter will make you a better problem-solver because it gives you the tools to do a better job of evaluating that information.

The Process of Researching

In starting the research process, you need to be able to locate reliable, valid information. You should become familiar with knowing where to find and evaluate books and serials in hard copy as well as those subscribed to in electronic format. You also need to be able to evaluate other resources found on the World Wide Web and know that most of these resources should be used with caution.

Be Able to Locate Reliable, Valid Information

What is reliable, valid information? Where do you find it? We as a society are engulfed in information these days. The problem we encounter is determining how to wade through this deluge of information to find what we need.

Students always come to us totally mystified and confused as to what information they should use. Their instructor has told them "You can't use the Internet for your resources." Their librarian has told them to make sure they use the electronic resources (e-resources) found online. The students say, "But my professor told me I cannot use the Internet for resources. Aren't the e-resources on the Internet?" These conflicting instructions can be very confusing. Let's sort it all out.

Become Familiar with Three General Categories of Resources

Think of research resources as tools you will use to find information. We have divided the resources into three general categories: Traditional, reserves, and electronic.

- *Traditional resources* are those items found, for the most part, in the library setting. They include paper (hard copy) versions of books, journals, magazines, newspapers, and publications. Other traditional resources are microfiche, videos, slides, CDs, and any other media types.

    The non-traditional student, who is not as computer literate or savvy as others who have used computers since grade school, prefers to use traditional resources. This reluctance to use e-resources is disappearing quickly. Once non-traditional students find out how easy and convenient e-resources are to use, they prefer them to traditional resources. Using traditional resources is fine, as there will always be the need for them. To be information literate, however, you must to learn to use the variety of resources available to you.

- *Reserves* are handouts, notes, books, and other items that the professor asks to be available for students to use in a special location. These items have a shorter loan period. Students can check them out for one hour, three hours, or as long as overnight. Sometimes the items are put in *closed reserves*, which means they can't be checked out but must be used on the premises. The professor wants to make sure that all the students in the class have access to the resources.

- *E-resources* (electronic resources) are information you use on a computer. In the information age, you can find an abundance of information in electronic format *online,* which means via the Internet. In fact, many universities offer classes via the Internet. If you are an online student, you most likely will be doing *most* of your research online.

  Why are e-resources becoming so popular? Many students prefer using virtual (online) resources so that they don't have to lug heavy books around. Another reason students are using e-resources is that most of these resources are available 24/7. With an Internet connection, you can look for information on your computer at home day or night. The electronic format makes searching for information very easy. The important issue, though, is to make certain that you are using the correct e-resources and getting reliable, valid information.

Know Where to Go for Information

Universities and colleges offer several options on how to get information on the research resources available to you. Following are a few places where you probably can find this information.

- The information packet mailed to students at the time of acceptance. Make sure you read through any mailings you receive from your school. Information on what resources are available along with your login and passwords for those resources are usually found in this information.

- The new student orientation, usually held a few weeks before classes start. The orientation can be anywhere from one day in length to a week and can include pre-testing for class placement, along with student advisor information, class schedules, and information about available resources. You should make the effort to attend orientation.

- Freshman success classes. Freshman are usually required to take these class offered by the school, where they learn study skills, time management, test-taking skills, money management, and the resources available for research.

- Library research class. Because of the overwhelming amount of information and the increase in types of formats in which you can find information, most schools now offer a semester- or term-long library research class. We consider this class one of the most valuable and urge you to take it. Not only will you learn about the resources available to you; you also will learn how to use them.

- The library. Find out where the library is located. Most libraries have handouts and tutorials about the resources and how to use them.

Begin Your Research

To research a topic for a paper, begin by looking for appropriate books. Most research papers require you to find some of your information from books. Books give a more in-depth and varied coverage of a subject than do other resources, such as magazine or journal articles. The book you choose should

- Contain information that is relevant to your topic.

- Be current. Check publication dates. Make sure the material in the book is not dated (old). When you are looking for information about government policy in the 1990s, for example, you don't want to grab the first book you find on government policy and call it good—especially if it was written in 1976.

Hard Copy Books

You can find hard copy books in a library by searching its online catalog, discussed later in this chapter. Make sure that you know how to search for books by author, title, subject, and keyword. A staff person in your library can show you how to use the online catalog, or the library will have tutorials available for you. If you are not sure how to navigate the online catalog, make the independent learner in you take over. Click the Help menu. Then take the time to read some hints on how to conduct a search. If you still are having problems, ask for assistance. The library staff is there to help you.

Electronic Books

In the information age, books are becoming more and more available in an electronic format online. These books are usually found in the electronic resources available at your library. Additionally, the "information deluge" has brought with it several e-book vendors with their databases. Some common names you will see associated with e-books are

- Netlibrary

- Jones E-global

- Questia

- Ebsco

The most important thing for you to do is to find out from your librarian which e-book database(s) your school has available for you. Associate the name of each database with e-books. You also can buy e-books from book vendors online such as amazon.com and barnesandnoble.com.

The great thing about e-books is you don't have to lug a book around with you. When you are reading for leisure or entertainment, you probably will want a paperback or hard copy book to read while relaxing. When you are researching a topic, though, you most likely won't be curled up on the couch with your book in hand. You will be looking for specific information on your topic. Using e-books allows you to read the book on your computer screen. You don't have to worry about losing the book or not getting it back on the date it is due. Most e-books check themselves in, and you just check it out again if you aren't finished with it. Actually, you don't have to check it out; you can choose to browse through it instead.

Vendors such as Netlibrary have tools available for you to use while you are reading the book. Most will have a dictionary in the database so you can look up definitions of words you do not understand. Netlibrary has a Note feature that we like. You can click on the Note feature and then you can take notes as you read. If you use the Note feature, you can keep track of where you are in the book if your reading gets interrupted. When you come back to the book, you can remember where you were by looking at your notes.

Regardless of the e-book source your school uses, you should know what the source is, how to access it, how to find a book, and how to read that book online. You should also be able to use the tools that e-book sources have available. Once again, check with a member of the library staff to discover the type(s) of e-books available for you to use and how to access that information. The school library should have tutorials in hard copy or "how-to" information online that gives you step-by-step instructions on accessing and using e-books. You should be able to search for e-books from your online library catalog.

Become Comfortable with Using Serials in Your Research

Serials are publications that come in sequence or order, including journals, magazines, and newspapers. You will hear professors say you must get your information from a juried publication or a peer-reviewed publication, or the resource may be not only juried or peer-reviewed but also one that is found in the electronic database that the school subscribes to. Don't panic. It isn't that difficult. We discuss the differences between serials and what is meant by *peer-reviewed* and *juried* in a later section. Differences among serials can be determined using the following criteria:

- Type of publisher
- Audience
- Qualifications of author or authors
- Level of coverage
- Bibliography or references
- Format
- Advertising
- Indexed

Many publications have the word *journal* in their title, but that doesn't mean they are true journals. They are true journals only if they include scholarly research. The publications that do not include scholarly research are known as *trade journals*. The following sections discuss three types of periodicals and their characteristics: scholarly or research journals, magazines, and professional or trade journals.

Scholarly or Research Journals

Scholarly or research journals have these characteristics:

- May be juried or refereed; that is, an editorial board of experts (the author's peers, hence the term *peer-reviewed*) examines the articles before publication to ensure the quality of the article.

- Published to foster ideas and present new ideas.

- Usually published by institutions of higher education.

- List author's affiliations and credentials.

- Target other researchers or scholars in the field as its audience.

- Contain articles of primary research (research done by the authors themselves) and include a methods section describing how the authors went about conducting the research.

- Include extensive bibliographies or reference lists for articles.

- Contain little or no advertising.

- Often arranged as paginated volumes. (For example, if one issue ends on page 230, the next issue will start on page 231.)

- Have an abstract (brief summary) for each article to help the reader evaluate the article and decide whether it is worth using in the research process.

- Often have narrow focus on a specific subject area.

- Indexed in subject-specific indexes or databases.

Magazines

Magazines, published for interest-specific audiences, may or may not have quality material. They are not taken as seriously as scholarly journals. Their main purpose is to generate subscription and advertising sales. Magazines have these characteristics:

- Published by commercial publisher.

- Target audiences by demographics—age, gender, interest, and so on.

- Usually does not provide authors' credentials.

- Is never primary research, so no methods section is included.

- Does not provide bibliography or reference lists.

- Does not refer articles.

- Contains colorful, attention-getting ads.

- Does not provide abstracts of articles.

- May be indexed.

Professional or Trade Journals

The titles of these publications have the word *journal* but do not include scholarly research. These are "do it yourself manuals" for professionals and practitioners. They can resemble both scholarly journals and magazines.

- Published by professional or trade organizations, such as the American Library Association.

- Audience is usually other professionals or practitioners.

- Author's affiliations and credentials are usually given.

- Limited advertising, directed to a specific trade or profession.

- No bibliographies or very limited bibliographies.

- Sometimes contains primary research (JAMA) or secondary research (American Libraries).

- Articles are not refereed.

- Indexed in subject and general indexes or databases.

Hard Copy Serials

Schools and universities usually have several hard copy journals, magazines, and newspapers available. If you are searching for peer-reviewed journals in hard copy in the library, pay attention to the criteria listed earlier. This is where those critical thinking skills come in. Take the list with you and try to find peer-reviewed journals on your own.

To find articles in hard copy serials, you will need to find an index. An *index* is a separate book, journal supplement, CD, or listing that provides accurate references to articles in a number of different serials. The index in the library can be in hard copy, on CD, or online. Many serials have indexes, each with its own features, but they have some characteristics in common. You can search indexes by authors or by subject. Some indexes include abstracts (brief summaries) of the contents of each article. Ask a library staff person what indexes are available and where those indexes can be found.

After you locate the indexes, you can look for the articles. If you need information on gun control, for example, you can look up gun control in the index. Under the words *gun control* is a list of the articles that contain information on gun control. The list gives the article title, author, journal or magazine containing the article, and the date of its publication. When you have a list of articles you want to read, take that list, go to the serials section of the library, and locate the journal or magazine you need. When you have found the articles, photocopy them, read through them in the library or at home, and highlight the information you plan on using in your paper. **Do not** highlight the information unless you photocopy the article. Librarians do not appreciate you highlighting the magazines and journals.

Electronic Resources

Terms such as *Internet resources* and *electronic subscription resources* can confuse students. The confusion arises from the fact that most universities and schools now have journal, magazine, and newspaper articles available in full text from electronic subscription resources, or electronic databases as some are called, that are online. If the *New England Journal of Medicine* is available from ProQuest, for example, you can search for a journal article in that database. You can choose which articles you want and then either read them online or print them out to read later. The school subscribes to these resources by paying a fee for the use of the service. (This is where some of your tuition money is going.) Because not everyone has access to these resources, you will hear them referred to as "the invisible Web." You can use the Internet to get to the Web site of ProQuest, for example, but you can't use its resources without a login and password. The resources are part of the Internet but not available to everyone. When a professor tells you not to use Internet resources, he is asking you not to just go to Google or Yahoo and use a key word search for information. He is telling you to use the reliable resources your library has available for you to use.

The logins and passwords for electronic resources are usually found in orientation materials you have been given, in a freshman orientation class, or in materials that were sent to you when you became a student. If you didn't get that information, contact your school library and ask for information about the services available for library research. The staff member will get you in touch with the right person. Some of the most well-known electronic resources are ProQuest Direct, InfoTrac, EBSCONET, FirstSearch, and E-global, to name just a few.

To complicate matters a bit, most electronic resources have several databases available, depending on what your school has subscribed to. If your school has ProQuest, for example, it may have purchased ABI/INFORM, a database containing journals and magazines geared to the business community and students needing business-oriented materials. Nursing schools usually purchase databases that contain medical journals and medical information. If you are a nursing student, select the medical database that contains the information you need, rather than searching all the databases available. The great thing about most electronic resources is that you can limit your search. By either clicking on a check box found on your search page or by clicking on Advanced Search, you should be able to search for only peer-reviewed or juried articles, for articles by date (articles published after 2000 only, for example) or for journals in specific publications. Limiting your search in those areas will make your search for information much easier.

Once again, if you aren't sure where to find these resources, ask a library staff member. If you are on campus, you will usually find that libraries offer some type of class on library research or offer seminars or workshops on using the resources. A member of the library staff usually visits a freshman orientation class to give students information on available resources. You can ask a staff member for help or use the services of the academic coaches or tutors. Whether you are conducting your research at home or in the library, Remember that most electronic subscription databases have a Help menu. The Help menu will give you some pointers on basic searching and other helpful ways to find the information you need. Most university libraries have a link to all the electronic databases on their library Web page. They more than likely will also have an E-mail Your Librarian link on the Web page. When in doubt, ask someone for help. Get in touch with a library staff person at your school and find out how to access those resources. Then learn how to use them.

Search for Information in Online Resources

When you are trying to find magazine articles in an electronic subscription resource, you will want to become familiar with the databases in that resource. For example, when schools subscribe to electronic databases, they can choose different types of packages. For example, if you are attending a school that offers degrees in business, one of the databases selected will no doubt be a business package such as ABI/INFORM that will give you access to several business journals and magazines. If you are getting a nursing degree, your school will provide databases where you will be able to find medical information. An example would be Cinahl from OCLC, which is a database that allows students to search for articles and information in the nursing field. Schools usually purchase databases that provide information for all their academic programs. You will want to become familiar with such databases. If you aren't sure, use those critical thinking skills, and either ask for help or click on the database listing to see all the databases available from that service and what is contained in that database. Don't be afraid to click on buttons and find information. If all else fails, find the word HELP and click on it. It will tell you what you need to do to find information.

Following are some basic search tips that work in most electronic databases. Again, if you don't understand how to do a search, seek help in your library or click on the Help link that will give you some searching advice. If all else fails, remember to click on the Help button.

- **Use quotation marks (" ") to search for exact phases.**

- **Use more than one word in your searches.** If you are looking for an article about poisonous snakes, for example, don't just search for *snakes*. First, you will get way too many *hits* (results). Second, you then would have to read through the hits, hoping to find the word *poisonous*. Search for "poisonous snakes" instead. If you are looking for poisonous snakes from Brazil, try searching for "poisonous snakes in Brazil."

- Use a *Boolean search*, a search that contains *operators* (words that broaden or narrow your search). Boolean searches use these words:

  - **AND.** When you use the word *AND* in a search, the database finds *all* the words. In a search entered as "economics and war," for example, the database looks for an article containing both those words.

  - **AND NOT.** When you use the words *AND NOT*, the database finds articles that have the first word, but not the second word. A search entered as "Internet and not HTML," for example, finds just "Internet."

  - **OR.** When you use the word *OR*, the database finds articles with any of the words. A search entered as "Internet OR intranet," for example, finds articles containing either of the two terms.

While many other types of Boolean searches are available, those listed are the most commonly used. For other advanced searching tips, use the Help menu within the specific database. For more searching tips, try this Web site:

http://www.herts.ac.uk/lis/help/tutorials/dbbasic.html#focus

Use Interlibrary Loans

Sometimes you might find a book in a reading list or hear about a book that you know will be helpful in your research, and then find that it isn't available at your university or school library or the nearest public library. Ask a library staff member at your school whether an interlibrary loan service is available. Many universities have that service available for students as a free service, while others may charge a small fee.

The same is true of articles. While you are searching for a journal article, you might see that it is available only as an abstract or summary. Again, take the bibliographic information (title of journal, article title, and date of publication) to the librarian and request an interlibrary loan.

Approach the World Wide Web with Caution

We are not going to explain the entire Internet concept to you. We only want you to understand the differences in where you can find resources and the reliability of the information they offer. Here are the important points to know:

- The Internet is a way of connecting computers to each other so that they can exchange information.

- Before the development of the World Wide Web, computers exchanged information via Telnet, which transferred only text files.

- Now we have the World Wide Web, which is all the pretty little Web pages and pictures, and text that you find at Web addresses. The World Wide Web is just part of the Internet.

Even some instructors get confused when they say you can't use Internet resources or Web resources. What they actually mean is that you need to use the resources provided to you by your university or college library. Your instructors don't want you to just base your research on Web sites because that information may not be valid or reliable. Anyone can have a Web page. Iona Information can put anything she wants on a Web page. Does that make the information correct, reliable, or valid? Not necessarily. If you are pro-gun control, for example, you can create a Web page and post inaccurate statistics on it. You can claim that 1,000 people died last year from gunshot wounds in Rapid City, South Dakota, when only three people died from gunshot wounds. If students use that inaccurate statistic in their papers, their papers are inaccurate. You want your information to be as unbiased and reliable as possible.

The most important statement about researching that we can make is this:

The resources you should use most of the time are those available to you through your university or public library—the subscription electronic resources. Only as a last resort should you use Web resources that are not subscription resources.

Does that mean that none of the information on the Web is reliable and valid? No. The top-level **domain** part of a Web site's address can tell a lot about the legitimacy of the site. Sites ending in

- .edu are links to individual student Web pages.

- .org are nonprofit organizations.

- .gov indicate governmental departments or agencies.

- .mil are U.S. military organizations and are reliable for statistical information.

- .com are commercial sites, online services, or for-profit businesses.

- .net are networking and business organizations.

Some sites, especially those in the .gov, .net, .edu, and .mil domains (and even some .com sites), have some reliable, valid information.

Let's say you have found most of your information in books, e-books, journals, and magazines, in both hard copy and in electronic format. You also may have found a Web site with some information that wasn't found in your other sources but you feel you want to use it for your paper. There are some very simple guidelines to follow when deciding if you should use a Web site for information. Below are some guidelines and questions you can use to determine whether information on Web sites is valid and reliable.

- **Is the information accurate, reliable, and error-free?** To find out, ask these questions:

  - Can the information be verified?

  - Are sources listed?

  - Does it have authority?

  - Who wrote it?

  - Are the author's qualifications or background listed?

  - What are the author's qualifications?

  - How reputable is the publisher or organization?

  Web standards to ensure accuracy are still being developed, so being aware of the possibility of inaccuracy is very important.

- **Is the information objective?** Ask these questions:
  - Is the information presented with a minimum of bias?
  - Is the information trying to sway the opinion of the audience?
  - Is it personal opinion?

  The goals of those presenting the information are often not clearly stated.

- **Is the information current?** Ask these questions:
  - Are dates provided that indicate when the information was written, posted, and updated?
  - Is the information up to date?

  The publication date should be clearly labeled.

- **How thorough is the coverage?** Ask these questions:
  - What topics does the site address?
  - Are the topics explored in detail or depth?
  - Is the Web coverage different from the coverage in print resources?
  - Are you having difficulty determining the extent of the Web coverage?

- **Is the Web site itself reliable?** Ask these questions:
  - Has the site had an enduring presence on the Web, or does it suffer from the "here today, gone tomorrow" syndrome?
  - Can the site itself be altered by unknown parties?

Library Research Conclusion

Just reading through this chapter puts you well on your way to becoming information literate. Do you know all the answers? Certainly not, but you will be more comfortable as you use the library and its resources to research topics. You will be able to find the information you need from a variety of resources, evaluate that information, and use it in the correct way. Keep your site addresses for your e-resources handy. Get in the habit of using them instead of those in the .com domain. If you feel lost or don't understand something, remember to ask for help.

Best Practices Summary
Do's and Don'ts of Success Secret #7 Library Research

Do

- Do become information literate.

- Do know what is good information and where to find it.

- Do find out what resources your school library has available.

- Do know how to access electronic subscription database resources.

- Do ask for help if you need to see your school librarian or an academic coach.

- Do know what style or format should be used in writing your paper.

- Do know how to cite correctly—find out what style you should be using.

Don't

- Don't procrastinate getting started on your research.

- Don't get discouraged when looking for information—ask for help.

- Don't use a non-subscription Web site unless it is a last resort and you evaluate the site.

Success Secret #7 Assignment 1:
Conduct a Library Search

In you are an on-campus student, find the answers to all the following questions. If you are an online student, answer only questions 11 through 16.

1. Where is your university or college library located?

(continued)

(continued)

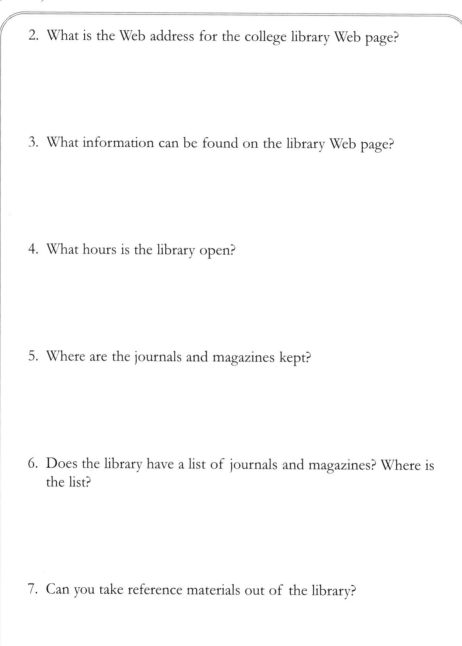

2. What is the Web address for the college library Web page?

3. What information can be found on the library Web page?

4. What hours is the library open?

5. Where are the journals and magazines kept?

6. Does the library have a list of journals and magazines? Where is the list?

7. Can you take reference materials out of the library?

8. Can you take magazines out of the library?

9. What is the borrowing period for books?

10. How many books can you check out at one time?

11. What is the Web address of the online catalog in which you can search for books on a computer?

12. What electronic subscription database resources are available for you to use?

13. Where can you find the Web addresses for those resources?

(continued)

(continued)

14. Where can you find the logins and passwords for those resources?

15. Does your school library have tutorials or students guides on how to use those resources? If so, where can you find them?

16. Does your library have an interlibrary loan service?

If the librarian was unable to visit your class, then you have to use those wonderful critical thinking skills and find the answers to those questions on your own. Go to your school library and find a staff member who can answer the questions. If you are an online student and do not have a campus near you, find out the address to the library Web page and find out the answers through viewing the Web page. If you can't find some of the answers, email the campus librarian. When you have the questions and answers put down on paper, you will have the information available to you when you get ready to do your research.

Wow! That is a lot to find out. But not only do you need to find the answers to those questions; you need to learn how to use those resources as well. Motivate yourself: Tell yourself you want to learn these things because you will not only be a better student, you will be very successful at doing your research. Get a classmate to help you find the answers. Learn how to use the resources together.

Success Secret #7 Assignment 2: Search the Web for Library Skills

Go to the Web site that lists the nine information literacy standards for student learning:

http://www.broward.k12.fl.us/learnresource/Info_literacy/ 9_standards.htm

Then answer these questions:

1. Do you consider yourself to be information literate? Why or why not?

2. What do standards 3 through 6 mean to you? (Explain your answer in a written paragraph.)

3. What do standards 7 through 9 mean to you? (Explain your answer in a written paragraph.)

CHAPTER 8

Success Secret #8: Research Papers

*"Whatever you attempt, go at it with spirit.
Do what is expected—and then some."*

Anonymous

Many students have been out of the academic setting for a long time. You may be one of those who have forgotten some of the basics of writing a research paper. We are going to give you a very basic outline to help jog your memory and get you started down the right path to the correct way to write a research paper. This chapter presents some of the most important aspects about the process of writing a research paper and some dangers to avoid. Let's begin the journey of writing a research paper.

The Process

You must complete several tasks before you can turn your paper in. Many times you will see students writing papers in a computer lab, and you might be rather surprised at the writing techniques they use. Many write as they read the information for their papers. You might also see many writing with no information; they find their resources to cite after they have written their papers.

Here is a little-known secret: Professors actually read your papers and they know when you don't use the resources you are citing. As you will read in later sections, they also can tell whether you actually know what you are talking about or are just copying something from a source. So follow the process. Doing so will make your life much easier, and your grade will reflect that you followed the process. The tasks in the process include

- Determining a topic

- Finding, reading, taking notes on, and sorting information

- Crafting a thesis statement

- Preparing an outline

- Writing a rough draft

- Polishing a final draft

Decide on the Topic

Deciding on the topic of your paper may be the easiest or one of the most difficult steps for you. If your instructor assigns the topic, you can immediately begin your research. If you are responsible for selecting the topic, you have a decision to make. This principle can make it easier: The topic of your research paper should relate to the class in which the paper has been assigned. In other words, if you are writing a research paper for an economics class, don't turn in the paper you used for a humanities class unless you can relate it to economics.

This is a second principle: Your topic should be narrow enough to be manageable. The topic of capitalism, for example, is very broad. The topic of economics during the Reagan administration, however, is much more manageable.

If you are confused about the topic of your research paper (and other issues, such as content and grading), ask your instructor. Instructors sometimes give students ideas on appropriate topics for research papers. If you still aren't sure, seek out an academic coach or tutor for guidance.

You also can find books that list topics for research papers. Check out the school library to see whether it has copies of those kinds of books. One of the better ones is *10,000 Ideas for Term Papers, Projects, Reports and*

Speeches: Intriguing, Original Research Topics for Every Student's Need by Kathryn Lamm (Arco Publishing, New York). If you are in a four-year degree program, this book might be worth buying.

The Public Affairs Information Service of Online Computer Library Center (OCLC) has a Web site that has some excellent hot topics in the research area. Go to this site, and click on the Recent Hot Topics link:

> http://www.idebate.org/database

A third principle is that you conduct a few quick searches to make sure that you can find enough information on the subject to write a paper before you waste time on a dead-end topic.

Take Notes

Taking notes is an important part of research. You will use your notes as the basis of your paper. Follow these tips to taking notes on research:

- **Use index cards of different colors so that you have a quick way of identifying their content.**

- **If your subject has three main ideas, color-code the information in three categories.**

- **Be very accurate in writing down statistics and direct quotations.**

- **Write down major points and pertinent information on your cards.** You should also write down where you found the information, using the correct citation format, as you take notes.

This chapter gives general ideas for writing a research paper. If you really want to brush up on your writing skills and basics of writing a research paper, check out an exciting writing lab at Purdue University, Online Writing Lab (OWL), which is available online at http://owl.english.purdue.edu/lab/.

Your paper should consist of no more than 10 to 15 percent quotations. In other words, you have to find the information, read it, analyze it, and put it in your own words.

Sort the Information

After researching your topic and taking notes, the next step is to gather your notes together, sort through them, and organize the information you have gathered, grouping the cards into common subtopics or themes. When you do that, you will begin to see a direction to take your paper.

Write the Thesis Statement

A *thesis statement* is the question you propose to answer in the paper. Remember these basic points about a thesis statement:

- **Keep it simple.**
- **Make it specific by narrowing the subject.**
- **Make sure that your research supports your thesis statement.**
- **Ask your professor to approve your thesis statement.**

Create an Outline

The purpose of an outline is to help you think through your topic and to organize the information before you start writing. Your outline should include an introduction, the body, and a conclusion, following these steps:

1. Write an introduction at the top of an outline. Your introduction should include statistics related to the paper or information that will get the attention of those who read your paper. The introduction should also clearly state your thesis and the purpose of your research paper. Why are you writing the paper? Explain briefly the major points you discuss in the paper.

2. Write the body, listing the arguments that support your thesis statement.

3. Write the conclusion, which is a restatement of your thesis statement, summary of your arguments, and an explanation of why you came to this conclusion.

Write a Rough Draft

Do not fall for the temptation to turn in the first version of your research paper. Enter the process accepting the fact that the first sentences and paragraphs you write will form a rough draft. To begin your writing, follow these steps:

1. Start with the first topic in your outline.

2. Read the notes that coincide with the first item.

3. Summarize the main idea expressed in the note, and paraphrase or use quotations for every idea you plan to use.

4. Read your paper and check for grammar and spelling errors, using the grammar and spell check features in your word processing program.

5. Have an academic coach or tutor proofread the paper for you.

Prepare the Final Draft

When you are satisfied that you have written an interesting introduction, a well-organized body that supports your thesis statement, and a conclusion that recaps the thesis statement in a unique way, you are ready to prepare the final draft. Make sure that you follow these tips:

- **Type your paper on a computer.** (You probably are thinking that that is obvious, but you might be surprised at how many students turn in handwritten papers.)

- **Revise your paper, making any changes, running spell check, and having someone proofread it.** Use the academic coaching or tutoring service for a proofread.

- **Completely reread your paper.**

- **Go through your paper once more to make sure you didn't miss any errors or grammar mistakes.**

After you have finished writing and are ready to print out that final draft, proofread, proofread, proofread. Use spell check and grammar check in the word processing program to check your paper. However, remember words may be spelled correctly, but you could possibly have the wrong word. When you type the word *their* rather than *there*, for example, the computer program won't pick up on the fact that you used the word incorrectly. Also, you may have typed a sentence twice or moved some text around and left some of it behind. Make sure the paper has a nice flow and that it all makes sense.

Some tutors will proofread papers for you and make suggestions on how to improve what you have written. That doesn't mean they are going to rewrite your paper. It means they will guide you by giving you suggestions about grammar, flow, and other details.

Important Issues in Writing Research Papers

Some of the most important issues discussed by professors and those who work in or with academics are cheating, plagiarism, and correct citation format. Once again, rest assured that professors do read your papers, they do pay attention to format, they do know whether you are plagiarizing, and they do know whether you cheat. Please make sure you read this section carefully and pay attention to which style of citing information is acceptable in your school, make sure that you don't plagiarize or cheat, and learn how your success could be drastically affected if you don't take the following information seriously.

Use the Required Style

Make sure that you write the paper in the correct format or style. What is the correct style? It depends on which university or college you attend or the style your instructor prefers. Most universities or colleges and/or instructors state the style that students should use when documenting resources. Find out the style your school and instructor prefer. Most likely, you will use American Psychological Association (APA) or Modern Language Association (MLA) style.

The APA style is the writing style described in the *Publication Manual of the American Psychological Association*. Many other disciplines, such as sociology, business, economics, nursing, social work, and criminology, use the APA style. For more information on this style, see:

http://www.apastyle.org/

Scholarly manuscripts and student research papers use the MLA style. It concerns itself with the mechanics of writing, such as punctuation, quotation, and documentation of sources. For more information on MLA, see:

http://www.mla.org/style

"Cite Right"

After reading an article, you probably will want to refer to it in your paper. You can do this in two ways: You can either directly quote the passage, putting quotation marks around it, or paraphrase it, using your own words to restate the article. You don't want a paper full of quotations, so you should try to paraphrase as much of the information as possible.

Whether you quote or paraphrase others' writings, you need to cite your sources. Most school libraries have a handout, library Web site, or a book that shows how to cite your sources (also referred to as citations). A citation merely tells your audience where you found the information in your paper. Then you must put in parentheses at the end of the information where you went to find the information.

The following example, taken from a book on writing, uses the APA style. It is a short, direct quotation written by multiple authors.

> "Any piece of information not set off with quotation marks must be in your own words. Otherwise, even though you name your source, you plagiarize by stealing original phrasing" (Reinking, Hart, & von der Osten, 1999, p. 385).

On the citation page at the end of your paper, you give additional information on where you read that quotation or where you got the information for your paper. Following is the correct format for the citation at the end of the paper:

> Reinking, J., Hart, A., & von der Osten, R. (1999). *Strategies for Successful Writing* (5th ed.). New Jersey: Prentice-Hall.

The citation indicates that the source of the quotation is a book written by multiple authors.

The formatting of citations varies, depending on the type of resource. Book citations differ from citations for magazine or journal articles, for example. If you are using electronic resources, use the citation format for electronic resources. If you are using paper resources, use the format for paper resources. Get the publication date right. If you aren't sure how to "cite right," get some help. Ask a librarian, an instructor, an academic coach, or a classmate. For further information on correct citation, see the Web sites mentioned earlier.

Make sure you use the style required by your instructor—for a couple of reasons. First, using the wrong style can seriously affect your paper's grade. Second, correct citations make it easy for your instructor to check your sources. Writing your paper in the correct format and citing your references correctly does take a little extra time. However, when you have written your paper in the correct format and used the correct citation format once, writing the next paper correctly will be easier and less time-consuming.

Cheating and Plagiarism

With all the things you have going on in your life as a student, sometimes you may be tempted to take the easy way out of writing a paper: You may consider buying a paper or getting someone else to write one for you. Buying a paper already written is blatantly **unethical**; it is **cheating**. You are turning in a paper that you didn't write and getting credit for it.

Plagiarism is a significant problem at the university and college level. Many students do not know they are plagiarizing. Following are three results of copying or using other people's words without citing correctly:

- The person who actually wrote the original work doesn't get credit.

- The person who plagiarizes is getting credit for work that he or she didn't do.

- The person reading the paper may not be able to check the original source and cannot rely on the information.

Following are two rules for making sure you don't plagiarize:

- Any fact, idea, or opinion that is not originally yours and not common knowledge must be cited.

- Anything you need to look up is not common knowledge.

Trust us. You will feel better if you write your own paper. After you do all the research and write a few papers, *you* are the person who becomes information literate. Read the articles and books you have gathered for your research. When you decide what information to use, try to summarize it in your own words. Make sure you let your instructor know where you found your information on the citation page. If an instructor can't locate that information, you won't get the credit for it.

Once again, instructors are very aware that students can buy papers. They also are aware that students sometimes take shortcuts. Computer programs and subscription services are available for faculty to use that will tell them whether you bought a paper or plagiarized someone else's work. In fact, universities and colleges pay for those programs and services, which mean they are very reliable. Please trust us when we say that most instructors will read your papers, they will check your resources, and they will know if you cheated or plagiarized. Don't take the chance of getting a zero on a paper or on flunking a class. Do your own work.

Research Papers Conclusion

Writing a research paper is not an easy task. I hate to use the old cliché of "practice makes perfect," but it is true. The more papers you write by following the correct process and learning the correct citation format, the more successful you will be as a student. Do your best, remember to use your support system, and get help if you need it. By doing your own work and doing it correctly, you will feel more positive about yourself and your grades will reflect your success.

Best Practices Summary
Do's and Don'ts of Success Secret #8
Writing a Research Paper

Do

- Do know what style or format should be used in writing your paper.

- Do use the correct resources subscribed to by your institution for mining information.

- Do use current information.

- Do follow the steps outlined earlier in the process of writing your paper.

- Do ask your academic coach or tutor to proof your paper.

- Do write in third person and check your verb tenses.

- Do know how to "cite right," using the required style so that your paper is formatted correctly.

(continued)

(continued)

> ### *Don't*
>
> - Don't plagiarize or use someone else's paper.
> - Don't write your paper without doing your research first.
> - Don't procrastinate writing your paper.

Success Secret #8 Assignment 1: Explore Types of Research Papers

In this assignment, you learn more about the types of research papers you may be required to write. Complete these steps:

1. Go to OWL at:

   http://owl.english.purdue.edu

2. Type "research paper" in the OWL Search textbox.

3. Scroll down until you see the Research Papers: Types of Research Papers link.

4. In a document, list the different types of papers and give a brief description of each.

Success Secret #8 Assignment 2:
Learn to Deal with Writing Anxiety

In this assignment, you research the topic of anxiety related to writing. Complete these steps:

1. Go to OWL at:

   http://owl.english.purdue.edu

2. Scroll down to the link for general writing concerns

3. Scroll down and find the Coping with Writing Anxiety link.

4. List three suggestions you found helpful or interesting.

CHAPTER 9

Success Secret #9: Synergy

"One horse can pull 2 tons, but 2 horses can pull 42 tons."

George MacDonald

Synergy is defined as the combined or cooperative action of two or more agents, groups, or parts that together increase each other's effectiveness. Just as the quote often attributed to George MacDonald states, we can accomplish much more when we have synergy, or help, than we are capable of doing alone. It is a truth that two heads are better than one. In fact, two heads can often synergize and do many times the work of one person, just as the horse analogy indicates. A critical secret for student success is recognizing the fact that you need others' help to be a winner.

Relationship Styles

What is your style of relating to others? Are you a Lone Ranger? Do you recognize the rich resources your cohorts can be for you? Do you accept and use all that others in your life can offer you? How savvy are you about creating and using relationships effectively?

The Lone Ranger

Are you a person who usually goes it alone? Do you get assignments and feel you have to tackle them by yourself? Do you feel uncomfortable asking people to assist you when you are stuck? Then this chapter is for you.

Even the Lone Ranger wasn't really alone. He had his trusty sidekick, Tonto, and his horse, Trigger. Students aren't alone either. Despite the fact that you may initially feel alone, classmates, instructors, technical support personnel, student services mentors, and a host of others are available to assist you with literally every question imaginable—if you seek their help. And the best way to synergize with any number of these people is to ask!

Cohorts

You need support from others in your classes. With a little know-how and practice, you can find emotional and intellectual bonding in your class. But how?

When you feel as if no one is out there, reach out to instructors or other students. All instructors have office hours. If you can't find a convenient time to see an instructor, send e-mail or leave a voice message. And remember this: Other students probably feel as alone as you feel. Ask for classmates' e-mail addresses or phone numbers. Don't be afraid to get connected to instructors or fellow classmates. (If you are an online student, you probably will find that people open up even more because they have a sense of anonymity.)

The Others

Many students readily recognize that fellow students and instructors related to their education offer synergism. However, few see the people directly in front of them—family, friends, and co-workers, just to name a few.

Once again, ask for help. Whether you are asking family and friends to help care for your children, elderly, pets, or other responsibilities, ask. People in your circle can make your life easier while you're getting an education; use them. Let someone pick up your kids. Let someone cook for you. Let someone help you.

Can you exchange services? Perhaps you can type fast. Can you exchange typing a friend's paper for help with childcare? You don't have to write the paper; just type what he or she has already written. When you understand the power of synergy, you know that no matter what problem might occur, you can ask for help, and a solution will be found. Ask.

The Win-Win of Synergy

Many of us hesitate to ask for help. However, on more than one occasion, after people have helped us, they have told us that, by requesting their help, we have actually helped them. We cannot guarantee reciprocal help, but we want you to see the opportunity your asking for help gives others.

Synergy involves the simple concept of sharing. Sharing what you are learning helps reinforce what you have learned. Be willing to help another classmate (not cheating, but student mentoring). Become involved with fellow classmates. Ask them what they are getting out of the course, and you will find valuable perspectives. Interact with other students so that you can gain new, fresh ideas important to your studies. How can you synergize your life? The following sections discuss these methods of activating synergy in your life:

- Be assertive.

- Keep an open mind.

- Be personal.

- Network and share.

- Don't bail.

Be Assertive

Students should speak up and take initiative when they are having difficulties. If you are an online student and the Internet technology is not working, for example, let someone know. Getting online should not be difficult. Don't waste time trying to figure out that which you do not know. Many schools have free 24/7 tech help available. Find out and keep the tech help number and e-mail address near your work desk. Remember, the squeaky wheel gets the grease.

The same can be said for on-campus students who are working in a computer lab. If you are having trouble getting a printer or an application program to work, find someone who works in the lab, look for an academic coach, or even ask someone else you see working in the lab.

It's also important to remember people can't read minds. If you don't ask, others can't help you. If you don't know whom to ask, pick someone and ask whom he or she would ask for answers.

Keep an Open Mind

Be open to learning new things. Just because you haven't used the applications in your school computer labs or some type of media doesn't mean you can't learn how to do so. If you aren't sure how to get started, ask for help.

After you have asked for help, you may get some seemingly off-the-wall answers to your questions. Don't immediately reject any answer until you prove it to be of no help. It is important to remember that ideas and opinions are not necessarily good or bad, just different and within the realm of possibility. Many great inventions came from seemingly off-the-wall ideas and answers. The Wright brothers, Thomas Edison, and Albert Einstein are just a few people who had or were given off-the-wall answers that were not rejected. Thank goodness for that!

Be Personal

It is very important in the classroom environment to be personal when asking and answering questions, especially if you are e-mailing a question. Successful students will tell you to address people by name or title. Many people assume that most e-mail messages are junk mail and automatically delete them. However, when you send an e-mail with the person's name and/or title, he or she is much more likely to answer you.

Here is a tip for online students: Use the other learners' names in class discussions. Also, reference the topic and sign your name to your posts. Doing so makes threads much easier to follow. Find our how your instructor prefers to be addressed and then use that name.

Network and Share

Networking involves seeking professional relationships with your class-mates, instructors, and school staff. Networks provide strength and resources.

Readily sharing tips and suggestions for success is often referred to as the "glue" in networking relationships. You don't have to reinvent the wheel. Others may have already invented it or know where to find it. Reach out to them and synergize.

Don't Bail

If you are not doing as well as you hoped, stay in touch with your instructor and the class. Ask your instructor whether academic coaches or tutors are available for your class and ask for their contact information. Most tutoring services offered by the school are free. Ask whether any of your classmates would be willing to assist you. (You can offer to pay for the call if you are an online student, but they might help you through e-mail.)

Above all, ask for help when you do not understand a concept. Instructors cannot read your mind (at least, most cannot). If you have questions, ask! Most course content builds concept upon concept. You might miss out on an entire concept because you failed to ask for clarification. Successful students advise others to use all the resources available.

Here is a tip for online students: See whether your online class has a built-in electronic library and search engines available to you. This could be a library Web page or include electronic resources such as ProQuest, NetLibrary, and others you learned about in Chapters 7 and 8. Most schools do have such resources, and you will get your own password to use them.

Above all else, don't quit. If you are doing something you believe will make your life better, don't quit. A popular saying you will find to be true among your classmates and many others states, "If you have never felt like quitting, then you really weren't running the race." The point is that nearly everyone has felt like quitting at one time or another. If you haven't, you probably aren't even running the race. Don't give up. Walk or crawl if you have to, but finish the race. It's a race you started. It's a race worth finishing!

For Online Students

Unlike a traditional class, an online class depends upon e-mail and bulletin board postings for all class and instructor interactions. Checking into your class frequently will ensure that you stay informed of the important things going on in class.

It is easy to feel isolated when you never see another person's face; however, you are not alone. Be sure to ask questions if you need clarification. Though you cannot go to your instructor's office in person, most online instructors have office hours, where you can reach them in real time by phone or e-mail. E-mail often provides you with quick responses day or night and even on the weekend, when most students are doing their homework. Being an online student is far from being isolated or cut off—unless you choose to make it that way. You just have to communicate in a different way online.

Learning online is a different type of learning experience than traditional classrooms provide. Be open to learning through a new medium and try not to accept preconceived ideas about learning online.

Synergy Conclusion

Synergy is defined as the combined or cooperative action of two or more agents, groups, or parts that together increase each other's effectiveness. And now that you know what synergy is and how valuable it can be, you have no reason for not implementing this best practice. You can harness the energy of others through synergy, which is essentially a principle of success that states, "You should never go it alone." You need to allow others to participate in your process and in your life, dreams, and goals. Your effects won't just double; they'll increase exponentially. Try using synergy, and you will see many miracles come to fruition in your life when you worth with others and let them help you.

Best Practices Summary
Do's and Don'ts of Success Secret #9 Synergy

Do

- Do seek help from your classmates. They are in the same boat as you. Row together and make sure you ask where the restroom is.

- Do seek help from your family, friends, and co-workers. These people are often initially overlooked, but they want to help you succeed. When you succeed, so do they.

- Do see asking as win-win. Those from whom you seek help are often helped themselves.

- Do be assertive. The squeaky wheel gets the grease. Some great online student advice is to step up and speak up.

- Do have an open mind. You may get some very unique advice when you ask for it. Don't immediately discount any idea as bunk.

- Do be personal. E-mails should always begin with the person's name. The sweetest sound in the whole world is your own name, whether spoken or typed.

- Do share and network. Your class is a great place to network. If you don't share, we guarantee you won't be able to network.

Don't

- Don't go it alone. If you do, it will be a very tough road to graduation— much tougher than it has to be.

- Don't be afraid to ask. FEAR stands for "False Expectations Appearing Real." If you are afraid to ask, you will be afraid to succeed.

- Don't quit. Never give up. It's as easy and as difficult as that!

Success Secret #9 Assignment 1: Conduct a Web Hunt for Synergistic Ways to Win

Go to the following Web sites and find three ways that you could use to increase synergy in your own life. Be prepared to share these with your class.

Synergy

> http://www.profitadvisors.com/synergize.shtml

Team building

> http://ianrpubs.unl.edu/misc/cc351.htm

> http://www.adventureassoc.com/team/teambuilding.html

Success Secret #9 Assignment 2: Create Synergistic Networking

Practice the principles in this chapter by completing the following steps.

1. Find out and record the names and e-mail addresses of three of your classmates:

   Name _____

   Address _____

   Name _____

   Address _____

   Name _____

   Address _____

2. Send an e-mail to each of your instructors, introducing yourself. Record the instructors' names, the dates you sent the messages, and the dates they responded.

Instructor's Name _____

Date Sent _____

Date Responded _____

Instructor's Name _____

Date Sent _____

Date Responded _____

Instructor's Name _____

Date Sent _____

Date Responded _____

Instructor's Name _____

Date Sent _____

Date Responded _____

Instructor's Name _____

Date Sent _____

Date Responded _____

Instructor's Name _____

Date Sent _____

Date Responded _____

CHAPTER 10

Success Secret #10: Motivation

"The secret of getting ahead is getting started."

Often attributed to Mark Twain

It has been said that you need to be a self-starter to be successful. In any classroom situation, being a self-starter will only enhance your success. If you don't consider yourself a self-starter, don't despair. You can learn how to take action and become self-motivated. *Motivation* is a willingness to perform a certain action (in other words, taking online classes or enrolling in college) for a real or perceived reward such as a college degree, a better career, more money, or class flexibility (evenings, weekends, online, or accelerated classes). When you take these actions and create the reward statements, you will find it just as easy to become motivated to register and complete online courses as jumping online to check your personal e-mail.

Success Principles in Motivation

It is a common misconception that people are born self-motivated. This myth can actually have some truth until we recognize the success principle of motivation. Simply put, the success principle of motivation is based on the premise of wanting to do something.

The statement, "I want to start classes this fall so I can graduate and get a better job," and the statement, "I have to start online classes this fall so I can graduate and get a better job" look very similar, but they are *not* the same. The only thing we all "have to do" in life is die some day. Everything else is a choice.

By replacing the words "have to" with the words "want to," you prime your subconscious to process your tasks as desirable and motivating. In other words, you create a reward system linked to your behavior regardless of whether you truly "want to."

Success Secret #10 Assignment 1: Change the Messages You Send to Your Subconscious

Complete the following tasks.

1. List five tasks that you don't really want to do related to online education.

_____

_____

_____

_____

_____

2. Rewrite the five tasks, beginning with the words, "I want to."

_____

_____

_____

_____

_____

3. Repeat the list in step 2 every day for 21 days. Soon you will find yourself motivated enough to become a successful self-starting student.

An example of this assignment follows.

1. I "want to" learn how to use the computer so I can be successful in online classes and get a degree that will earn me more money.

2. I "want to" spend 10 hours a week in each of my online classes so I can maintain at least a 3.5 grade point average and have the best chance of getting into law school.

3. I "want to" organize my office/computer area and always keep it neat and clean so I can maximize my online class efficiency and effectiveness.

4. I "want to" take a typing course so I can be more efficient in online classes and spend more time with my family.

5. I "want to" take the online orientation course before I take my first class so I can be more proficient and successful.

The reality may be that you feel you "have to" learn to use the computer, or spend 10 hours a week in each online class, or organize and keep your office/computer area neat and clean, or take a typing class, or take an online orientation course. However, by telling yourself that you "want to" do these things and justifying them with appropriate rewards and outcomes, you are creating a fertile atmosphere for self-motivation. You will notice a difference.

Visualize the Reward

Find your desire in succeeding with your classes. Get in touch with the "Big Picture." Go to the future in your mind and ask, "How will my life look different on the outside when I successfully complete my classes?" For example, can you see yourself in your desired career as a powerful, highly successful employee or entrepreneur? Perhaps your life is filled with multiple new possibilities and choices for yourself and others.

The reason to visualize the reward is that learning can seem like a maze you "want to" go through to get the cheese. The goal, of course, is to visualize the reward and *want* to go through the maze to get the cheese. If you focus on the cheese, you will become inspired and self-motivated before and during the journey.

Overcome Motivation Roadblocks

Inevitably, you will run into roadblocks in getting your education. By using the tools and best practices of your time management in Chapter 11 and organization in Chapter 4, you create a new path around, over, or underneath the roadblocks in your online journey. It has been said, "The only difference between stepping stones and stumbling blocks is how they are used." We believe this statement to be true, and so do hundreds of successful students. In fact, some of the most common stumbling blocks, such as time limitations and disorganization, can easily be remedied. The secrets to success identified in these chapters will empower you when you get stuck or off-track so that you can get quickly back on track and moving toward your goals.

Build on Small Victories

Get familiar with the class structure and your instructor. You need to learn how to navigate and become acclimated to your surroundings. The more time you spend getting comfortable in the platform, the more time and energy you have available to devote to succeeding in your actual course work.

When you have successfully completed a class, pat yourself on the back. This is a small victory that you can use to build significant motivation to propel you through your course curriculum.

Balance Your Life

Balance is another identified key to success as a student. We must not underestimate its importance primarily because of the frequency with which students focus their sole motivation on course and degree completion, while neglecting other areas of their lives.

To prevent this "tunnel" motivation, you might want to map out how you are doing in the key areas of school, work, health, family, finances, spirituality, and social life. If you ignore any one of these areas, you will get out of balance, potentially sabotaging your success. According to Dr. Wetmore's time-saving article on his Web site, "If you fail to take time for your health now, you will need to take time for illness later."

Successful students remind others to get plenty of rest and eat well. You are fueling the engine from which your work flows. It is vital to fuel your engine so you can be excited and interested in the material, instead of waiting for others to make it interesting for you.

Surround Yourself with Winners

Surround yourself with people who want you to win and believe in you. Keep in mind that it takes 11 positive people to undo the negative energy of 1 negative person, so stay away from negative, fault-finding people as much as possible. They will systematically take your enthusiasm and motivation from you. Stay strong and surround yourself with people who also want you to succeed.

Instructors are sometimes unable to motivate students. However, those of you who are self-motivated and self-disciplined have a unique benefit that provides you with the independence and opportunity to work at your own pace. The convenience of being self-reliant gives you the flexibility you need to be successful.

Motivation Versus Enthusiasm

Hundreds of very successful motivational speakers travel the country each year. They are paid well by a variety of corporations and social organizations to motivate employees to perform, produce, and invent. Many companies invite the speakers back year after year because of the results attributed to their motivating the people who attend.

The reality of motivational speakers is that very few actually motivate people. Rather, they create an atmosphere of enthusiasm similar to that of a sports pep rally. They often talk about changing the world, and indeed we have been to many motivational seminars and felt the very same way after the speech. However, that feeling or desire to change the world quickly faded as the hours moved past.

The reason for this phenomenon is that most motivational speakers are actually "enthusiasm" speakers. They create a short-term intense feeling of change, creativity, and drive. However, unless the speaker can connect individually with each person in the audience, the concept of long-term self-motivation will never manifest itself into action.

It is easy to feel enthusiastic about succeeding in your classes after reading this book. In fact, many students will be raring to go before completing all the chapters. We simply want to emphasize that our goal of your success in obtaining your degree is reached through perseverance and self-motivation. Remember, you can earn your degree in less time if you are self-motivated. Completing a degree is more than a short-winded sprint that requires only temporary enthusiasm.

Self-motivation results from a conscious perceived reward or benefit attached to behavior and performance changes. It's the typical carrot in front of the horse analogy. However, if the horse doesn't get a bite of the carrot every now and again, he will quit walking. This is precisely the stance successful students take for generating self-motivation. Each successful assignment, quiz, or project is like taking a bite from the carrot in front of them. It motivates them to walk a few steps further until the course is successfully completed. A few more carrots—make that classes—and you have the reward and/or benefit.

Motivation Conclusion

After reading this chapter, we advise you take time to do a personal inventory and decide whether you can be self-motivated (largely a decision based on habits rather than an innate behavior). You are in charge of your own life. You choose whether to apply the principles of creating an atmosphere of motivation in your life. If you cannot choose to change your habits to motivate yourself, success may more difficult. You will be working against yourself. Learn to go with the flow.

Best Practices Summary
Do's and Don'ts of Success Secret #10 Motivation

Do

- Do visualize your reward. Focus on your goals of taking college classes. It's easier to become motivated when you use visualization.

- Do have realistic expectations. Expectations of rewards for behavior are what drive motivation. Make sure your expectations are realistic and not just a pipe dream.

- Do move around motivation road blocks. Use time management (Chapter 11) and organization secrets (Chapter 4) to turn stumbling blocks into stepping stones.

- Do balance your life motivation. Don't forget to continue your motivation for good health, happiness, and family harmony.

- Do surround yourself with winners. Water rises to its own level. Surround yourself with winners and positive people, and you will become one too.

- Do say, "I want to" rather than "I have to." Remember this key success principle as you do the things that are less than fun.

- Do build on small victories. Use victories of completing an assignment or the orientation class to motivate yourself to complete your degree.

Don't

- Don't confuse enthusiasm with motivation. Enthusiasm is short-term excitement; motivation is long-term energy tied to realistic expectations and rewards.

- Don't lose your motivation focus. Periodically review your goals and their associated rewards.

- Don't blame others for your lack of motivation. You are in charge of yourself, your thoughts, and your actions.

Success Secret #10 Assignment 2: Conduct a Web Quest to Find Tips on Motivation

Complete the following tasks.

1. Go to the following Web sites or choose your own through a search engine:

   http://www.geocities.com/academicsuccess/motivate.html
   http://www.oaklandcc.edu/iic/iicah/ah_www_sss_col.htm

2. Find three tools or tips you could use to motivate yourself or others in a constructive manner.

3. Be prepared to share these with your class.

CHAPTER 11

Success Secret #11: Time Management

"The only reason for time is so that everything doesn't happen at once."

Albert Einstein

Remember that you are accountable for managing your time. Accept full responsibility for your schedule. If you blame others for what you seemingly "have to do," your life will stay stuck in a helpless mode. To move to the life you want, you must take control and responsibility for your time. If you need to pick up your children, for example, recognize that that is your choice, and you will have more energy if you acknowledge that reality. It is your life and your opportunity to succeed or fail. You get to decide. Remind yourself of this concept on a daily basis.

The Keys to Time Management

Do you know how to manage your time, or do you always feel as if you're playing catch-up? How can you find the time to do all the things you need to do? We have some simple but powerful keys that can help you unlock the door to hours in your days.

Plan Ahead

You want to rid yourself of the notion that "there is always tomorrow." If something is going to be accomplished, it will be because you made it happen, either consciously or by default. Planning your time leaves less up to fate and chance. Decide on a plan to allocate and balance your time: family, job, school, and social activities. Decide what you want and need to do each week and plot it all out. Without a plan, you can easily get distracted and off-track.

We have this note of caution: When planning ahead, don't over-plan. Allow some things to resolve themselves—and, trust us, they will. When you pre-plan everything, you put life in a box. Quite frankly, life is much more fluid than that. You want to allow opportunities for "Ah ha" experiences to work in your life, and for that to happen you need some breathing room. So in essence, have a plan, but don't become so rigid that you block out the easier or more enjoyable ways to accomplish your goals.

Learn When to Say "Yes" and When to Say "No"

Be true to your word. Say "No" when you mean "No." Say "Yes" when you mean and want to say "Yes." To maintain balance in your life, you will want to say "No" to some things. However, you also want to say "Yes" on occasion to gain new experiences and perspectives that may directly benefit your learning experience. If you say "Yes" too often and spread yourself too thin, you are reducing the energy allotted for your educational goals. Remember, guilt goes away, while resentment does not.

Avoid Procrastination

Procrastination is habitually putting off things that you should be doing. If that sounds like something you do, pay special attention to this section. There is hope.

Avoid procrastination at all costs! It can make you miss deadlines and create an unpleasant experience. Procrastinating can also cause a great deal of stress that actually inhibits learning. When you are concentrating on catching up, odds are you are not absorbing the information in class, leading to other problems down the road.

One key to avoiding procrastination is to stop using the words "have to." When you say, "have to," you are actually starting the procrastination process. Your subconscious starts thinking of ways that it does not "have to." You end up fighting yourself, and the procrastinating process begins. Instead, tell yourself the reasons you "want to" do something. You want to study to pass the test. If you pass the test, you pass the class. If you pass the class, you are closer to receiving your degree. You "want to" do your work now so you don't need to do it later. You want to; you do not have to. Actually, in this world you don't have to do anything but die. Almost all else is a choice when you get right down to it. The words you tell yourself will start changing your behavior. Be very careful with the words you use.

The second key to avoiding procrastination is to not allow others to take over your study time. This is another reason to have a set study time. Your family and friends will less likely sidetrack you if they know your study schedule in advance. On the flip side, you don't always want to neglect others, either. Rather, try making a win-win arrangement for all concerned. You can do this. Reward your family and yourself for keeping to your study schedule. When you study at the times designated and you do well on your exams or assignments, treat yourself to extra time with friends or family or do something fun for an hour or two. You can take in that movie you wanted to see or take the kids to the park.

Establish a New Routine

The reason you want to study at a certain time on a regular basis is that doing so trains your brain to know that now it is time to focus and absorb knowledge. Establish a dedicated time for your studies and develop the habit of doing your studying at a certain time on certain days so your brain will become ready to absorb knowledge.

Prioritize

Another time management secret to being a successful learner is the ability to prioritize. People who don't know how to prioritize become procrastinators. A big part of effective time management is being able to set priorities so you can keep on track with everything you have to do surrounding your responsibilities inside and outside of being a student. Even if you are busy, you can schedule your tasks, depending on their priority in your life. You should align your efforts with your goals and your life purpose. Doing so will cause you to put more priority on the important tasks rather than just the urgent ones. Steven Covey has many practical tools at the following Web site for the process of prioritizing:

http://www.dkeener.com/keenstuff/priority.html

Make decisions about what are your "babies." You can choose from among many ways to do this. One is to make a list of daily things you want to get accomplished and then mark or circle the ones that are essential to do that day. Then schedule the days and times in which to do your work and keep them as interruption-free as possible. This way, you give your coursework a high priority in your life and take it more seriously. Establishing your coursework as a priority will make you more successful than if you just sit down to study when you are "free."

You can make a separate list for personal items or make one list with all the goals of the day. You can also make a list at the end of your workday for the next day. That way, you can rest knowing that you will tend to details the next day with nothing being overlooked or forgotten. Keep in mind that, no matter how you slice it, you have 24 hours in a day to work with. Consider limiting your list to 10 items, with the 5 most important highlighted, and a timeframe for completion. Determine the activities in your day that are actually time wasters and eliminate them.

Another way to prioritize is to identify your top three or four items for the day and tend to them, rather than making a long list of less important things. Keep in mind that if getting the dry cleaning on the way home will increase the peace at home, that might be worth keeping on a list.

Some experts suggest making three lists: One that includes your long-term success goals; one that has urgent, but not as important things you want to accomplish; and one more list of things that are nice to do or have, but only if you have the time. The warning here from successful learners is to *not* spend so much time making lists prioritizing daily events and scheduling that you don't have enough time for your coursework.

Keep your to-do lists near your study area so that you can cross items off as you complete them. Humans are teleological: Once we make a goal, we seek to do it like a heat-seeking missile. In other words, if you consciously think about it, your thoughts and actions will gravitate toward your goals. Harness this aspect of your being.

Furthermore, you may want to put another list near you for your worries, but write at the top that you are shelving them or letting a power higher than you deal with them. We know people who write their problems on a list. When they go home at the end of the day, they leave the list in the mailbox so they can focus on their family. Then they pick up the list in the morning and take it to work with them. It is symbolic of letting go of things that you have no control over so you can focus on your goals, whether that is family time or studying.

An important part of prioritizing is learning how to "do the right things right." It is good to be efficient, but if you are being efficient at things that are not taking you anywhere, then really, what have you accomplished? Not much. Rather, the best practice is to learn how to be efficient at effective things. Your time is valuable. Put a price on it. Don't step over dollars to pick up dimes. Don't spend your time and energy on useless timewasters. Become less rigid about what you believe you need to accomplish. Just because you have always done something a certain way does not mean that it is the most effective, efficient method. Keep your eye open to shortcuts. Hang around people who seem to be "doing the right thing right" and ask them how they plan and strategize their time and life. Adapt new effective techniques in your life. If you don't, it is easy to become a "busyaholic" who is not producing much but looks busy and feels overextended. Many people are in the rut of rushing around in a frenzy and accomplishing very little. Yet their energy is spent, and they get up and do the same thing the next day.

To prevent the "busyaholic" time management practice, you should work and study smarter, not harder. You can follow the 80/20 rule. In other words, **20 percent of your efforts produce 80 percent of the results.** For more information, you can do an Internet search on "80/20 rule of time management." Following is one Web site you might find helpful:

http://www.aafp.org/fpm/20000900/76the8.html

Success Secret #11 Assignment 1: Personal Time Survey

Most experts suggest using the personal time survey tool if you truly want to have more "time" in your life. For 24 hours, plot your time on this chart so you can find the timewasters and holes that are wasting your precious energy. In the long run, this simple activity can significantly change your life. You will gain an amazing awareness because so many of our time management habits are unconscious. By having an awareness of how you spend your time and energy, you can start shifting that energy to effective and efficient activities.

Hours		Hours	
6:00 am		6:00 pm	
6:30 am		6:30 pm	
7:00 am		7:00 pm	
7:30 am		7:30 pm	
8:00 am		8:00 pm	
8:30 am		8:30 pm	
9:00 am		9:00 pm	
9:30 am		9:30 pm	
10:00 am		10:00 pm	
10:30 am		10:30 pm	
11:00 am		11:00 pm	
11:30 am		11:30 pm	
NOON		MIDNIGHT	
12:30 pm		12:30 am	
1:00 pm		1:00 am	
1:30 pm		1:30 am	
2:00 pm		2:00 am	

Hours		Hours	
2:30 pm		2:30 am	
3:00 pm		3:00 am	
3:30 pm		3:30 am	
4:00 pm		4:00 am	
4:30 pm		4:30 am	
5:00 pm		5:00 am	
5:30 pm		5:30 am	

After completing the personal time survey, it is often best to prioritize your schedule by looking a week ahead. When planning your week's schedule, include all your activities and look ahead to the following week. If the week ahead is jam-packed with deadlines and appointments that cannot be rescheduled, but this week is a light load, schedule time to do at least 50 percent of next week's studying this week. Also when the week is over, examine what parts of the classes took more time than you expected and allocate more time for those areas for the next week's schedule.

Start Early, Work Steady, and Finish with Time to Spare

One suggestion for making your own time schedule is to take a piece of poster board and tack it to your wall. On this board, you can mark spaces or time slots and map out a schedule that you would like to follow. You can use hours or half-hour time slots for a busy schedule. You can include other commitments as well, such as soccer games and doctor's appointments. Also add commitments such as classes, work, meals, and driving time.

Capitalize on your body rhythms and identify your biological prime time. Schedule your study time when you are at peak energy for it, and allow for breaks. This method enables others in your life to know what you would like to be doing or are doing on any particular day at any time. Another suggestion is to schedule your long meetings right before lunch or at the end of the day.

When you look at what you have scheduled, you can now ask yourself if you have enough time. Most likely your answer is that you do not. Don't be a perfectionist about this. Sometimes you should work toward perfection, but this is not one of those times. Use your time schedule as a goal. See whether you can find a way to take a few minutes off one thing and add the extra time to the things that mean the most to you. Find ways to combine activities. For example, listen to taped lectures while you exercise or while you are driving. What you have done is set forth a map to use as a guide.

Success Secret #11 Assignment 2: Describe Your Perfect Day

Now that you know what your day is really like and you have given thought to how you can actually construct it, you can take it a step further and raise the stakes a bit by doing this assignment. We are making this assignment because we believe the success tool that says, "If you can think it up, you can have it—with some effort, of course."

For this assignment, ask yourself, "When am I most energetic, happy, and excited about life? Am I a morning person, or is my energy better in the afternoon or evening? Where do I like to work—in an office, cubicle, or my home? For what type of a business do I prefer to work—how large or what type of organization? How long of a commute do I prefer? What kind of a boss or supervisor do I want, or do I want to be the boss? What am I earning an hour?"

In other words, spell out your preferences in detail. Write them down. Think about and write a description of what your life would look like if your concerns or problems were solved. Keep in mind that the details are significant here. We are asking you to make up a true story. If you make it vague, then you will get a vague life, probably not what you truly desire. Write it down and put it someplace where you can see it periodically. Be prepared to discuss your description in class.

10 Time Management Principles for Online Learners

The skills and habits needed for being a successful online student are different from those of the typical college student who attends courses in a classroom setting. These differences are why sharing success secrets is so important for online students. Furthermore, an understanding and integration of these secrets is necessary if an online student is to excel and overcome the unique challenges of online learning. Success assignments are included to ensure that you put these secrets into practice.

The first success secret needed for student online success is time management, a must if you expect to stay focused from week to week and have time to stay on top of the studies that you must manage for yourself. Online students cannot just procrastinate on projects, quizzes, and term papers. While it's not advisable for traditional onsite students to do that, either, most online courses close the week with a grace day or two and make missed assignments or quizzes unavailable. This time lag or "grace day" allows the instructor to grade your assignments. The familiar adage, "If you snooze, you lose" comes to mind in the online environment.

Just as each of you is unique, with your own unique priorities, commitments, and responsibilities, your ideal way to manage your time is going to reflect your individuality. Your goal is to have a relationship with your time that feels meaningful and valuable and enables you to meet the obligations of your professional life, family, and social life. You also want to have the time to take care of your most valuable asset—your health.

While we do not have a one-size-fits-all time management formula, we do offer some basic principles you can adapt to your special circumstances.

(continued)

(continued)

Principle 1: Your most important tool in an online class is your computer. You should use this time management tool to your advantage. One of the most important things to download and print is the online course syllabus—essentially, the contract between the instructor and you. The syllabus usually includes a summary of assignments, quizzes, tests, projects or term papers, case studies, and grading policies. Successful online students also download their weekly assignments and lectures and print them so they can work when they are away from "class" or the computer.

Principle 2: When completing assignments, quizzes, and so on, successful online students take the time to do it right the first time, saving them the time they would have spent redoing it. Conversely, if they make mistakes, they don't beat themselves up. Rather, they learn from their mistakes and move forward.

Principle 3: This is a seemingly opposite principle to "Doing it right the first time." That is, "Not all things are worth doing perfectly." For example, for you to type your grocery list and spend hours making sure that you know everything you will get before you leave the house is not a good use of your time. Make a "good enough" grocery list and get on with it. You will learn more about this principle in the discussion of prioritizing.

Principle 4: Create a plan to allocate and balance your time: family, job, school, and social activities. Asynchronous classes allow students to decide when and where to study and log in. Therefore, you want to make a time management plan that has enough wiggle room to allow for daily changes or emergencies.

Principle 5: Successful online students also recommend scheduling some recreation. Your goal should be to maintain a balanced life while taking online courses. Take inventory of the priorities in your life and where you feel you need to adjust. You can still have the life you seek despite taking online classes.

Principle 6: Set designated times on your calendar to go online each day and week so that you have it in your schedule. Remember that little bits and chunks of time add up. The recommendations for participation per week for most online courses average 8 to 15 hours. Go into your online class at every opportunity, even if you have only 5 to 10 minutes. You probably make time to check your personal e-mail several times a day, so start checking your online course e-mail every day as well. Jump on the bulletin boards, if only for a few minutes. Expecting to pull an all-nighter until the work is done is setting yourself up for a journey that may not be pleasant for your loved ones or you. In fact, most online schools require at least three different days per week of participation for full credit. With a little planning, the journey can be an enjoyable one.

Principle 7: Do your work when you are supposed to do it. It is easy to procrastinate online and easy to fool yourself into thinking that nobody really knows whether you log in or turn in your assignments. Of course, the reality is that electronic tracking systems are exceedingly accurate. The computer platforms can track when you log in, where you go in the class, what you submit, and how long you work in each area. Do not be fooled by thinking you can hide in an online class.

Principle 8: Do something in the right direction. Sometimes just getting started is the key to breaking the procrastination habit. There are some tools to assist you. An example of this is to do the one thing you do not want to do for five minutes. This is also known as the Five-Minute Success Rule. This will often be enough to break the procrastination. Set a timer and work for just five minutes, and then see if you can do five more. Often you just need to get started in order to succeed.

Principle 9: Do the things you don't want to do first. Get them out of the way. You can use typical procrastinating behaviors such as checking personal e-mail, playing Internet

(continued)

(continued)

games, or getting a snack as a reward for actually doing some work in your class. This way, your typical procrastinator behaviors become an incentive rather than a way to avoid working. And remember, if you fall behind, get back on track as soon as possible.

Principle 10: Accept the fact that your attendance will most likely be at odd hours. You will want to make it routine in order to create a new and positive habit.

Time Management Conclusion

In this chapter, we have adopted several methods of effective and efficient time management strategies from the comments of hundreds of successful students. Hopefully, you will find one or more of these best practices helpful in your success. Do not try to apply ALL of these time management practices. It is essential to not make time management scheduling, prioritizing, etc. monopolize precious time needed for coursework. Initially, it may take a few hours to develop a time management plan. But a good rule to follow during coursework is to spend less than two hours a week organizing your time.

Best Practices Summary
Do's and Don'ts of Success Secret #11
Time Management

Do

- Do allow time to absorb what you are learning. The ability to grasp a new learned thought will lead to a better understanding.

- Do make working on your class a habit. If you write down *when* you go online, you will not have to worry about forgetting whether you *did* go online.

- Do something for your class every day. That way, you aren't stressed by last-minute deadlines.

- Do get other *essential* non–course-related tasks out of the way before studying so that you aren't worried about all the things you have in addition to studying.

- Do take a break and relax. If you don't, you'll actually take longer to do the same amount of work.

- Do cancel, postpone, or decrease other commitments to free time for your courses. It pays off in better grades, increased knowledge, and less stress.

- Do start with the most difficult assignment. Your energy level needs to be at its highest for success with these sorts of tasks.

Don't

- Don't spend too much time organizing and scheduling your week. Don't walk over dollars to pick up dimes.

- Don't implement all time management techniques. Picking one or two that fit your life is sufficient.

- Don't fret over things for which you don't have time. Prioritize, delegate, and do what you can.

Success Secret #11 Assignment 3: Change Your Mind and Change Your Life

This chapter explained how changing your life from a "have-to" to a "want-to" basis allows you to get the changes you seek in your life. Usually time management is on a "have-to" basis. Most likely you have not changed your procrastination habits regardless of the electronic time management devises you have purchased.

In this assignment you will

- Apply what you learned in this chapter on time management skills.

- Identify your current time wasters.

- Research Web articles on time management. This could also include study skills and test-taking.

(continued)

(continued)

- Identify new tools for managing your time more effectively.

- Write five goals based on the new tools you would like to use in your life.

1. Look again at the 24-hour chart you created in Assignment 1 to give yourself a realistic picture of your current use of your time.

2. Find a total of three articles that present you with the tools for change that you want to use, using any search engine, such as Google or Ask Jeeves.

3. Write out your new tools in the form of three new time management goals.

4. Save all this information to share with your class.

CHAPTER 12

Success Secret #12: Stress Management

"Success is directly proportional to how much stress you can gracefully endure. When you can deal with stress with joyous productivity, your blessings increase."

Karine Blackett

Stress can be defined as the way we react, positively or negatively, to physical and emotional change. In the 21st century, we are living our lives under a great deal of stress. People complain every day that they do not have enough time to accomplish all they want to do. Most live very busy lives and can easily get caught up in those "stressful moments." Additional stress has entered in our lives since 9/11. Daily we receive a significant amount of negative news, and our lives just are not as simple as they used to be.

You as students not only have stress from society, jobs, family, and friends, but also from academic challenges. This chapter looks at the physical and mental signs of stress and causes of stress, and gives some great stress-reducing tips.

Types of Stress

Stress can be either positive or negative. Yes, there is such a thing as positive stress. The following sections discuss the differences between positive and negative stress.

Positive Stress

Positive stress, sometimes called "eu-stress," is like an adrenalin rush. It can help us attain difficult goals and can even enhance our performance. Positive stress can be energizing, motivating, and even lifesaving. A certain amount of stress can activate our creative subconscious and give us ideas on how to successfully complete tasks or solve problems. The human stress response fuels us for athletic events, pressures us to earn money, and even yanks us out of harm's way when we find ourselves in danger. Total absence of stress would make life boring.

Negative Stress

Negative stress, sometimes even referred to as "distress," happens when stress exceeds a certain limit. It detracts from performance. Negative stress can take its toll on both physical and mental health, causing many ailments. Physical ailments caused by negative stress can include

- ❑ Frequent headaches
- ❑ Ulcers
- ❑ Hypertension
- ❑ Backache
- ❑ Shoulder and muscle tension
- ❑ Allergies
- ❑ Asthma
- ❑ Fatigue
- ❑ Insomnia
- ❑ Liver disease
- ❑ Heart disease
- ❑ Stroke

- ❑ Lowered immunity
- ❑ Obesity
- ❑ Change in vision
- ❑ Pain that can't be explained
- ❑ Nail biting, nervous tics, flinching

Mental ailments caused by negative stress include

- ❑ Anxiety
- ❑ Inability to concentrate
- ❑ Lack of appetite
- ❑ Depression
- ❑ Fear
- ❑ General irritability
- ❑ Forgetfulness
- ❑ Insomnia
- ❑ Tearfulness
- ❑ Confusion

Causes of Stress

There are many causes of stress. In fact, you can have stress in every part of your life. Let's take a look at some of the major causes of stress, especially those causes that directly affect you as a student.

One of the biggest causes of stress is probably worry. Benjamin Franklin said, "Do not anticipate trouble or worry about what may never happen. Keep in the sunlight." As a student, you may have many worries. "Will I do well on my exam? Can I write a good paper? Can I go to school and still take care of my family?" You might ask yourself hundreds of questions daily that can cause stress. If you are an employee as well as a student, you might be worrying about the economy and your job. If you have a family to take care of, you might worry whether you are spending enough time with them while you are a student. You might be worried about a scholarship you need that will enable you to finish school. The list of the questions and concerns you have in your daily life could go on forever.

We like to think of worry as "what-if's." You know the common what-if's you worry about. We can "what if" ourselves to death. "What if I don't pass the test? What if I don't get that scholarship? What if I can't get the student loan? What if my family doesn't think I am spending enough time with them since I am now in school and working? What if job, school, and life just become too difficult?" What if, what if, what if?

Do you know that over 90 percent of those things we worry about never happen? Don't you feel better already? We can hear those sighs of relief from way over here. All areas of our life can be stressful. Let's take a look at the causes of stress in your personal life, in the workplace, and in academics.

Stress in Your Personal Life

Our personal lives can be the source of our greatest joys; they also can cause great stress. Do you have any of the following stressful events in your life right now?

- ❑ Marriage/separation/divorce
- ❑ Pregnancy/birth/death
- ❑ Personal injury or illness
- ❑ Loss of job/retirement
- ❑ Moving between homes/buying a house
- ❑ Changing jobs
- ❑ Change in financial status
- ❑ Relationship problems
- ❑ Change in eating/sleeping habits

Stress in the Workplace

Another source of great fulfillment is work. However, it too can be very stressful. Do you experience stress from any of the following sources?

❑ Promotion

❑ Threat of redundancy (dismissal from a job, especially by layoff)

❑ Change in working hours or conditions

❑ Low pay

❑ Feeling of lack of control

❑ Lack of job satisfaction

❑ Personal friction/office politics

❑ Heavy workload or long working hours

❑ Sensory factors such as heat or noise

❑ Racism, sexism, or ageism

❑ Meeting deadlines

Stress from Academic Pursuits

You enrolled in school to improve your future, but attending school can make heavy demands on your time, energy, and mind. Do you experience any of these academic-related stresses?

❑ Overcoming a poor academic record

❑ Maintaining a certain GPA

❑ Being out of your comfort zone

❑ Competition with other students

❑ Increased difficulty in subject matter

❑ Increased pressure from difficult assignments

❑ Looking for additional sources to finance tuition

Ways to Relieve Stress

It is very important to relieve stress as much as you can in your life. We probably cannot be successful in eliminating all the stresses in our life but we can reduce some of the stress.

Earlier chapters in this book have given tips for releasing stress when you are taking exams, and advice on maintaining a positive attitude.

Following those helpful tips will reduce some of your stress, but you should work on reducing stress in your life on a regular basis. The following sections give just a few quick pointers on how to reduce everyday stress, what we call the "stress busters."

Know Your Limits

Everyone's tolerance for stress is different, and every person handles stress in a different way. You will find it helpful to be aware of your stress limits.

Success Secret #12 Assignment 1: Determine Your Stress Level

Go to the following Web site and take a stress test. Find out how stressed out you really are.

http://www.stressbusting.co.uk/quiz/quiz.asp

Maintain Healthy Eating Habits

Nearly everyone is worried about weight, trying to find the quickest way of losing it. So many diets are out there today that deciding which one to follow is enough to cause stress. Doctors continue to recommend that we should quit all the fad diets and maintain healthful eating habits. This is good advice. Breakfast is still the most important meal of the day. You need fuel to think, and healthy food is fuel. "Eating healthfully" is a good habit. When you are "eating healthfully," you may take longer to lose those unwanted pounds, but you are healthier while you're doing it. If you have forgotten the infamous food pyramid and the types of food you should be eating, go to the following Web site, which gives some tips on maintaining a balanced, healthy diet.

http://www.health.gov/dietaryguidelines/

However, the pyramid also promotes eating a great deal of bread and grains. You, like others, may find that a "higher protein, lower carb" diet fuels your brain and body better.

Exercise

Experts agree that exercising is one of the best ways to relieve stress. Exercising produces endorphins, which can reduce pain naturally and give you a feeling of relaxation and wellbeing. Exercise also can reduce blood pressure and help you fall asleep faster. Not only does it have these great positive effects on your body; it also can give you a few minutes of time alone. Join an aerobics class, an intramural sports program, cycling, or weight training class, which involves about an hour, twice a week. Taking the time to exercise is worth it. No phone, no doorbell, no kids, no bosses, no instructors. Just a fifteen-minute brisk walk can not only reduce stress but help you keep in shape.

With your busy schedule, exercising may be difficult, but try to get into a regular exercise routine. Motivate yourself to exercise. Write affirmations about exercise, but don't forget to be very specific about when and what. Don't just write, "I exercise." You need to write "I eagerly exercise on Monday and Wednesday, taking a brisk walk at 1:00 p.m." When you write the affirmation positively, you tend to adhere to it. Not only write your affirmation, but remember that you *want* to exercise. Don't make it a "have to." To learn more about stress relief and exercise, go to this Web site:

http://exercise.about.com/od/healthinjuries/a/stressrelief.htm

Stay Positive

We can't stress (oh, there's that word again) enough that having a positive attitude definitely can help you reduce or even bypass stress. You *can* pass that exam. You *can* eat healthier. You *can* enjoy exercise.

Take Some Time for Yourself

Try to spend at least 10 to 15 minutes a day just on you. You can enjoy a cup of tea, light some candles, and just relax. A good time to do this is right after work or right after school. Take a little time from your day to let go of the day's stressful events before interacting with your family or friends. Then you can face those you care about with a good positive attitude. They will appreciate it. You can't use the excuse that you don't have time. Go back and read the chapter on time management again. If you absolutely can't make it a daily routine, you can find 10 to 15 minutes every other day to spend on you.

Make Time for a Hobby

Gardening, painting, crafting, or tinkering in your garage can be great for stress relief. Many people will say they don't have time for a hobby. Planting flowers or a garden can take a little time in the beginning, but maintenance of that garden or flower bed takes only a few minutes each day or even a few minutes twice a week and gives you that time you need to just relax. You can take a few minutes to work on a quilt or crafting project each day. There is nothing that says you have to finish a craft as soon as you start it.

Listen to Relaxing Music

The emphasis in this stress buster is the phrase *relaxing music,* not the hardest rock band in the world. You may think that type of music releases stress and relaxes you, but it really doesn't. Hard rock may be your favorite music, but save it for the Friday night head-banger's ball or to energize you for studying if that works for you.

While you are cooking dinner, fixing something around the house, or driving in your car, listen to peaceful, easy listening music. Instead of listening to the nightly news, try putting on some nice, quiet music. The news is only going to cause you more stress, especially these days. Nothing is going to happen that you won't be able to read about online or in the newspaper tomorrow morning. If the world comes to an end, you will find out about it. Pass on the news and opt for some quiet or inspiring music.

For more information on the benefits of relaxing music, visit the following sites:

http://stress.about.com/od/tensiontamers/a/musicrelaxation.htm

http://holisticonline.com/stress/stress_music-therapy.htm

Meditate

Meditation is another great way to reduce stress. Many methods of meditation are available. Learning to use them takes practice, but meditation is worth learning. After you learn how to meditate, you can do it for short periods of time—even right before you take a test. Meditating will help you to relax, and the stress of the day will melt away. A good Web site to visit if you want to learn an easy method of meditation is this one:

http://www.alternative-medicine.net/meditation/english.html

Take a 20-Minute Soak in the Tub

Soaking in warm water is a great stress reliever. Run a bathtub full of warm soapy water, light some candles, turn on some quiet music, and get in the tub. Just relax. Shut your eyes and think about the music you are hearing. Practice the method of meditation you learned.

Watch Bits and Pieces of a Favorite Movie

If you like movies and know which ones make you feel happy and uplifted, take a few minutes before you start to study or do an assignment to watch your favorite parts. You will feel good and be ready to conquer those assignments.

Treat Yourself to a Massage

Find a good masseuse in your town or city and treat yourself to a body massage about once every three months. It would be great to be able to do it more often, but massages can be a little pricey. Try to find someone who does pressure massage. It can be a little painful, but it puts you back into alignment as well as relaxing you. Pressure messages also can reduce headache pain and other annoying little aches and pains you may have.

Use These Additional Stress Busters

Look for other small changes you can make to your life that will reduce stress. Following are some that we use.

- Breathe slowly.
- Avoid alcohol and drugs.
- Be prepared.
- Develop your study skills.
- Copy important papers you need.
- Use time management strategies.

- Keep a calendar.

- Network to get help when you need it.

- Set goals.

- Stop saying "Someday" and "Maybe things will be better tomorrow."

- Avoid negative people.

- Stop negative talk.

- Believe in yourself.

- Visualize success.

- Develop a sense of humor.

- Smile.

- Don't think you need to do it all or know it all.

- Say "No" more often.

- Look at problems as a challenge.

- Take in the beauty of the day or night.

Stress Management Conclusion

You can choose which stress management tools to use to reduce your stress. Being a student and busy with jobs and family does cause a great deal of stress. Remember to "eat healthfully," exercise, and select other stress busters to reduce stress and make you a more productive and positive person. If you seriously want to learn more about stress management, go to the Web sites we have listed. You can also stop by your local or school library. It probably has audiotapes and videotapes on stress management. Hundreds of self-help books on stress management are available. You can check them out at no cost, and they can be very helpful in reducing stress. Just remember that managing your stress levels will make your life much easier and make you a healthier and happier person and a more successful student.

Stress management completes our analysis and compilation of the 12 secret best practices for student success. Now that you know the 12 best practices for being a successful student, you will undoubtedly be head-

and-shoulders above those who didn't take the opportunity to read them. Like any great recipe for success, we recommend that you take the ingredients and modify them to suit your particular life. The 12 success secrets will provide you with the foundation and all 12 of these practices are related to your total success. If you use them, you will have the tools to go beyond your expectations for learning. These tools should not only increase what you get out of your academic experience but also improve your success in everyday life.

We welcome your best practices in your classroom experience. Send your suggestions to us; we would like to include as many as possible in our next edition.

Best Practices Summary
Do's and Don'ts of Success Secret #12
Stress Management

Do

- Do know that stress can cause illness.
- Do recognize when you are stressed.
- Do maintain a healthy diet.
- Do exercise regularly.
- Do stay positive.
- Do synergize.
- Do choose some stress busters and use them to reduce everyday stress.

Don't

- Don't worry.
- Don't let life get you down. You have the tools for success. Use them.
- Don't go it alone.

Success Secret #12 Assignment 2: Try a Stress Buster

Complete the following tasks.

1. Write a brief description of how you feel right now.

2. Go to the following Web site and read the instructions on how to complete the exercise.

    http://www.alternative-medicine.net/meditation/english.html

3. Practice the meditation a few times.

4. Write a brief description of how you feel after completing the exercise.

5. Compare your Before and After descriptions. Did the meditation have a positive effect on you?

Success Secret #12 Assignment 3: Experiment with More Stress Busters

Complete the following tasks.

1. Go to the following Web site and read through the 50 "stress-busting" techniques it presents.

   http://www.montana.edu/wwwpb/pubs/MT200016HR.pdf

2. Choose the one that you feel most relevant to you.

3. For one week, write a daily affirmation that states that you are applying that technique to your life.

4. On the last day of that week, write a description of how the affirmation has affected you.

Web Sites, References, and Readings

Here is a critical-thinking tip for you: If you try one of the following Web links and you get an error or it tells you the page can't be displayed, don't despair. When using Web addresses, sometimes a page will give you an address that extends past the .com, .net, .org, etc. Those file locations to the right of the .com, .net, .org can sometimes change. If you can't get to the page you want, try erasing any part of the address that appears after the .com, .net, .org, and so on. For example, let's say that you want to get to the following Web site:

http://www.howtostudy.com/studtips.htm

This page is supposed to give some great study tips, but all you seem to get is an error message. Delete the /studtips.htm and just use this:

http://www.howtostudy.com

That address should get you to the page you need. Then you can do a search on the Web page for "study tips." (We learned this trick when we were trying to keep Web links updated on our Web sites.)

Following is another idea that may help you: If you really want to search for more information on any of the success tips we have given you, use Yahoo, Google, or another good Internet search engine. Type what you are looking for in the Search textbox. You should get a list of sites that can be helpful.

The sites listed in this appendix can be helpful to you in studying, stress management, test taking, attitude, and so on. Just remember: Don't use them for doing a research paper. What resources should you use for your paper? Use the electronic resources provided to you by the school you attend. We hope the following information will continue to help you in your goal of enhancing your academic success.

Chapter 1 Study Skills

Web Sites

http://www.prenhall.com/success/StudySkl/ssa.html—Study skills assessment

http://www.ucc.vt.edu/stdysk/checklis.html—Study skills checklist

http://www.mtsu.edu/~studskl/10tips.html—College survival tips

http://www.abacon.com/firstyearfocus/index.html—Surviving the first year of college

http://www.csbsju.edu/academicadvising/helplist.htm—Remember what you read

http://www.prenhall.com/success/StudySkl/notetake.html—Note-taking skills

http://www.english-zone.com/study/symbols.html—Note-taking symbols

http://www.psywww.com/mtsite/mindmaps.html—Mind mapping

http://www.mtsu.edu/~studskl/mem.html—Memory skills

http://www.howtostudy.com/studtips.htm—Study tips, test-taking tips, chemistry and physics study tips

http://www.stthomas.edu/academicsupport/helpful_study_skills_links.htm —Study guides

http://www.studyguidezone.com/—Study tips

http://www.mindtools.com/pages/article/newISS_01.htm—Learn how to do mind map

http://www.dushkin.com/connectext/psy/ch07/chunking.mhtml— Chunking tips

http://www.usu.edu/arc/idea_sheets/pdf/mnemonic_dev.pdf—Mnemonic
   devices

http://www.allsands.com/Science/mnemonicdevices_soa_gn.htm—
   Mnemonic devices for studying science information

http://www.richland.edu/james/misc/testtake.html—Math study help

http://www.eop.mu.edu/study/—Lists of information—study guides,
   dictionaries, math and science and writing help

Additional Resources

Fry, R. (1999). *The great big book on how to study.* Franklin Lakes, NJ: Career
   Press.

Kesselman-Turkel, J. & Peterson, F. (2003). *Note-taking made easy.* Madison,
   WI: University of Wisconsin Press.

Paul, K. (2002). *Study smarter not harder.* Vancouver, B.C.: Self Counsel Press.

Ritter, B. & Gilpin, B. (2001). *The adult student's guide to survival & success.*
   Portland, OR: Practical Psychology Press.

Roberts, L. & Pritchard, L. (2004). Skills give students a spring in their step.
   Times Higher Education Supplement, 0(1622): 25.

Robinson, A. (1993). *What smart students know: maximum grades, optimum learning, minimum time.* New York: Three Rivers Press.

Siegle, D. (2004, Spring). The merging of literacy and technology in the 21st
   century. *Gifted Child Today, 27*(2): 32.

Weathers, B. (2004, February). Learning to learn: Student activities for developing work, study and exam-writing skills, *Teacher Librarian, 32*(3):35

Yates, J. & Yates, C. (2004). Freshman study guide. *Campus Life, 62*(7): 50-53

Chapter 2 Test-Taking

Web Sites

http://www.prenhall.com/success/StudySkl/testtake.html—Test-taking tips from Prentice Hall

http://www.wwu.edu/depts/chw/student_health/publications/ test_strategies_info.pdf—Test strategies

http://www.testtakingtips.com/—Test-taking tips

http://www.d.umn.edu/student/loon/acad/strat/test_take.html—Test-taking tips

http://www.learningskills.com/test.html—Measuring test-taking anxiety

Additional Resources

Newman, E. (1996). *No more test anxiety: Effective steps for taking tests & achieving better grades.* Los Angeles, CA: Learning Skills Publications.

Razakis, L. (2002). *Test taking strategies and study skills for the utterly confused.* New York: McGraw-Hill Professional.

Chapter 3 Perception, Personality, and Learning Styles

Web Sites

http://www.metamath.com/lsWeb/dvclearn.htm—Learning styles assessment

http://www.humanmetrics.com/cgi-win/JTypes2.asp—Personality type assessment

http://www.mindtools.com/mnemlsty.html—Learning style information

http://typelogic.com/—Personality assessment information

http://www.humanmetrics.com/—Personality assessment information

http://www.learning-styles-online.com/overview/—Discussion on learning styles http://www.mindtools.com/mnemlsty.html—Information on learning styles

http://www.usd.edu/trio/tut/ts/style.html—Learning style information

http://www.colorquiz.com/—Color and personality

Additional Resources

Aiken, L. (1999). *Personality assessment methods and practices.* Cambridge, MA: Hogrefe & Huber Publishers.

Baron, R. (1998). *What type am I: Discover who you really are.* New York: Penguin Group.

Berens, L. & Nardi, D. (1999). *The 16 personality types, descriptions and self-discovery.* (1999). Huntington Beach, CA: Telos Publications.

Gale, L. (1998). *Discover what you're best at.* New York: Fireside Books.

Chapter 4 Organization

Web Sites

http://www.studygs.net/orgstr1.htm—Organizing study projects

http://www.muskingum.edu/~cal/database/general/organization.html—All types of organization skills for studying

http://www.lemoyne.edu/academic_support_center/orgstdy.htm—Organizing your study time

Additional Resources

Fry, R. (2000). *Get organized.* Franklin Lakes, NJ: Career Press.

Worthington, J. & Farrar, R. (1998). *The ultimate college survival guide.* Princeton, NJ: Peterson's.

Rich, J. (1997). *The everything college survival book: Everything you need to know to fit right in before you're a senior.* Holbrook, MA: Adams Media Corp.

Chapter 5 Goal Setting

Web Sites

http://www.mindtools.com/pages/article/newHTE_06.htm—Goal setting tools

http://www.mygoals.com/—Goal setting ideas

http://www.psychwww.com/mtsite/page6.html—Goal setting psychology

http://www.siue.edu/SPIN/activity.html—Goal setting for academic success

http://www.goal-setting-guide.com/smart-goals.html—Smart goals

http://www.mygoalmanager.com/goals/—Goal manager

Additional Resources

Blair, G. (2000). *Goal setting 101: how to set and achieve a goal.* Syracuse, NY: GoalsGuy Learning System, Inc.

Wilson, S. (2004). *Goal setting.* New York: Amacom.

Davidson, J. (1998). *The complete idiot's guide to reaching your goals.* New York: Alpha Books.

Koestner, R., Lekes, N. & Powers, T. (2002, July). Attaining personal goals: Self-concordance plus implementation intentions equals success. *Journal of Personality and Social Psychology, 83*(1):231.

Chapter 6 Attitude

http://www.lessons4living.com/attitude.htm—What is attitude?

http://emotiontoolkit.com/posthink.shtml—Positive thinking tool kit

http://ezinearticles.com/?Attitude-Is-The-Key-To-Success&id=12596—Attitude and success

Additional Resources

MacKay, H. (2001, October) The choice is yours: Don't let 'no' handicap you. *Providence Business News, 16*(24):23.

Marshall, E. (2000, February 25). Positive attitude reflects power of choice. *Triangle Business Journal, 15*(26): 16.

Pham, L. & Taylor, S. (1999, February). From thought to action: Effects of process versus outcome-based mental simulations on performance. *Personality & Social Psychology Bulletin, 25*(2):250.

Snyder, M. (1982). When believing means doing: Creating links between attitudes and behavior. In M. Zanna, E. Higgins, & C. Herman (Eds.). *Consistency in Social Behavior: The Ontario Symposium, 2*(pp. 105–130). Hillsdale, NJ: Lawrence Erlbaum.

Wagner, C. (2004, January-February). Health and happiness: The medical power of positive thinking is getting closer scrutiny. *The Futurist, 38*(1): 10(1).

Chapter 7 Library Research Skills

Web Sites

http://www.dushkin.com/online/study/dgen1.mhtml—Library research tips

http://w2.byuh.edu/library/researchtips.htm—Library research tips

http://www.ithaca.edu/library/course/organize.html—Organizing research

http://www.muskingum.edu/~cal/database/general/writing.html—Writing skills

http://www.muskingum.edu/~cal/database/general/problem.html—Problem solving and critical thinking

http://www.thinkquest.org/library/—Created by students for students

http://www.ipl.org/—Online library

Additional Resources

Ertmer, P. & Newby, T. (1996). The expert learner: Strategic, self-regulated, and reflective. *Instructional Science*, 24: 1-24.

Robinson, A. (1993). *What smart students know*. New York: Three Rivers Press.

Schunk, D. & Zimmerman, B. (1998). *Self-regulated learning: From teaching to self-reflective practice*. New York: Guilford Press.

Chapter 8 Research Papers

Web Sites

http://owl.english.purdue.edu/—Research paper advice

http://webster.commnet.edu/apa/index.htm—Guide for writing research papers

http://www.wisc.edu/writing/Handbook/PlanResearchPaper.html—Planning and writing a research paper

http://www.ruf.rice.edu/~bioslabs/tools/report/reportform.html—Help on writing papers

http://www.gc.maricopa.edu/English/topicarg.html—Topics for research papers

Chapter 9 Synergy

Web Sites

http://www.profitadvisors.com/synergize.shtml—Synergy

http://ianrpubs.unl.edu/misc/cc351.htm—Team building

http://www.adventureassoc.com/team/teambuilding.html—Activities for team building

Chapter 10 Motivation

Web Sites

http://www.ucc.vt.edu/stdysk/motivate.html—Motivational tools

http://gwired.gwu.edu/counsel/index.gw/Site_ID/5176/Page_ID/14139/
—Success tips

Additional Resources

Chandler, S. (2004). *100 ways to motivate yourself: Change your life forever.* Franklin
Lakes, NJ: Career Press.

Harrell, K. (2000). *Attitude is everything: 10 life-changing steps to turning attitude
into action.* New York: Harper Business.

Chapter 11 Time Management

Web Sites

http://www.ucc.vt.edu/lynch/TMActivity.htm—Time management activity

http://www.mindtools.com/pages/main/newMN_HTE.htm—Tools for
time management

http://campushealth.unc.edu/content/view/460/150/—Time management
tips

Additional Resources

Tracy, B. (2002). *Eat that frog: 21 great ways to stop procrastinating.* San Francisco,
CA: Berrett-Koehler Publishing.

Chapter 12 Stress Management

Web Sites

http://stress.about.com/—Stress-related information

http://www.stresstips.com/—Stress tips and assessments

http://www.pp.okstate.edu/ehs/links/stress.htm—Stress management http://www.trance.dircon.co.uk/—Advice on beating stress

http://www.siu.edu/departments/bushea/stress.html—Personal Growth
Tool: Demo at bottom of Web site for Meditation

http://www.mindtools.com/pages/main/newMN_TCS.htm—Stress tips

http://www.tuesdaytoasters.org/tips/relax.html—Tips on relaxation

http://www.healthyeating.net—Information on nutrition, food guides, and
health

http://www.prevention.com/—Healthy living

http://www.healthology.com—Health and wellness information—read
articles or watch videos

http://bcbsnj.myhealthyhorizon.com/—Health and wellness

Additional Resource

Truman, K. (1991). *Feelings buried never die*. Salt Lake City, UT: Olympus
Publishing.

Index